MW00945491

How to Get Kids To Behave

The Manual that was Supposed to Come with Kids

Richard O'Keef

Copyright © 2016 by O'Keef Publications LLC

All rights reserved including the right to reproduce this book or portions thereof in any form whatsoever.

Disclaimer: The reader must act responsibly and at his or her own risk when following the recommendations contained herein.

Published by O'Keef Publications LLC

Email: howtogetkidstobehave@gmail.com

ISBN-13: 978-1530283316
ISBN-10: 1530283310

Table of Contents

Chapter 1 - Introduction...1

   You Shouldn't Have to Go it Alone 9

Chapter 2 - Why Children Misbehave 11

   The Two Built-in Needs of Every Child.....................12

   Belonging...12

   Personal Power..13

   How Children Meet their Own Needs 13

Chapter 3 - What Doesn't Work 16

   Out with the Old...16

   Strict vs. Permissive...19

   Say Goodbye to Screaming...21

   The Problem with Asking "Why" Questions...............21

   The Child is not the Behavior 22

   Why Punishment Doesn't Work 23

   Words Have Power 25

Section 1 - Appling Principles 26

   Decrease Children's Desire to Misbehave and Increase their Desire to Cooperate 26

Chapter 4 - Principle #1 - Reward Good Behavior.............27

   Piggyback a Value 33

   No More Criticizing...35

Chapter 5 - Principle #2 - Ignore Annoying Behavior........36

   Give an Ignore Warning...38

Chapter 6 - Principle #3 - Spend Personal Time with Each Child..41

Finding Time 42

Distractions... 43

Activities 43

Eat Together as a Family... 47

Make Positive Deposits 49

Do Acts of Kindness with Your Children 55

Chapter 7 - Principle #4 - Acknowledge Negative Feelings 58

Chapter 8 - Principle #5 - Teach Life Skills................... 71

The Training Plan.. 76

Unveiling the Training Plan 83

Putting the Training Plan into Action 84

Assign Chores 88

Offer Choices 91

Make Your House Kid-Friendly 93

Teach Problem-Solving.. 94

Let Kids Make Mistakes 97

Chapter 9 - Principle #6 - Have Weekly Family Meetings 102

What Do We Do? 103

Chapter 10 - Making Rules 113

Teaching Respect 119

The Problem with "Don't" 121

Stopping a Behavior 122

Section 2 – Using Techniques...................................... 124

Responding to Unwanted Behavior.............................. 124

Chapter 11 – Enforcing Rules 125

Describe What You See 126

Use One Word 127

Express How You Feel 127

Act, Don't Talk 129

Grant a Fantasy 133

Offer a Choice 134

Problem-Solve Together 135

Give Advance Warning 138

Cooling-Off Period 138

Chapter 12 – When-Then Statements 140

Set Up a Bedtime Routine 143

Set Up a Morning Routine 143

When-Then Tips 144

Chapter 13 – "I Feel" Statements 146

Chapter 14 – Sibling Rivalry 149

Chapter 15 – Consequences 158

Offering Choices with Consequences 165

Chapter 16 – Stop, Redirect, Reward 168

Hitting – Stop, Redirect, Reward 170

The Child Ignores Your Request 171

Chapter 17 – Tantrums 174

About the Author 178

Notes 183

Chapter 1 - Introduction

Parenting can be frustrating. Sometimes the frustration gets overwhelming and parents wish they had somewhere they could turn to feel understood and get help and inspiration. Since parents typically don't have a lot of time on their hands, this place should have information that is short and to the point, easy to understand, easy to do, and most importantly, promise to contain advice that will have a positive impact on their children's behavior.

I have written this book to meet that need. I have compiled information that is important for all parents to know; information that will guide parents through the tough times and make their jobs meaningful and more enjoyable by improving their relationships with their children. This book will take the guess work out of raising children and give parents the skills they need to deal with the most common behavioral problems. I wish I had had a book like this when I was a young parent.

So what makes this parenting book different from all the others, and what makes *m*e think I can give advice to parents? Let me begin by telling you how I came to write this book.

Years ago, my oldest daughter and I decided to write a book about babysitting. We called it, *How to Make More Money Babysitting*. We built a website and sold the book online for a few dollars. It didn't do very well. We decided to make the book more appealing by adding a section called, *How to Inspire Good Behavior*. Our intention was to offer a book that helped young people prepare to become parents by practicing good parenting skills on other people's children while babysitting. Sales were still disappointing. Then one day, we received an email from a parent thanking us for writing an "amazing book". She told us that the section, *How to Inspire Good Behavior*, was "pure gold" and explained how applying the skills she learned improved her children's behavior. She said that she was astonished at how "incredibly quickly" it worked and how she literally had two new children. She thanked us for giving her "new tools to bring out the best in her kids".

My daughter and I were stunned. Were we targeting the wrong audience? Should we be focusing on parents? Are there parents out there who need, and are wishing they had new tools to bring out the best in their kids? And perhaps the most important question, could I do something to help?

I made a decision to find out everything I could about how to get kids to behave. I read books, magazines and blogs. I listened to CDs and watched videos. There's a lot of information out there – some useful, some… not so much.

What I discovered was fascinating. For many parents, the only way they know how to raise children is to do the same things their parents did – even if they *hated* what their parents did.

Many parents are like drill sergeants who bark orders at their children. They threaten, lecture, punish and scream. The problem with that is, it produces only short term obedience, not long-term cooperation.

Then there are those parents who practice the "permissive" style of parenting. The kids walk all over their parents because their parents don't like confrontation, or they just don't know what to do, or they're worn out from being drill sergeants. The kids grow up with an entitlement attitude. They think the world owes them.

Then there are the helicopter parents. They hover over their children to prevent their children from making mistakes. They shield their children from life's consequences. As a result, their children don't know how to think for themselves. They don't learn how to make decisions or solve problems. They don't learn from making poor choices. They are unprepared to meet the world when they grow up.

Many parents throw up their arms in frustration when nothing they do seems to make a positive difference in their children's misbehavior. They have discovered that love is not enough. They want to change their children's behavior but they don't know how. Some feel that if they just stay the course, somehow things will get better. But they learn that if they do nothing different, nothing changes. Others would welcome helpful information and set out to find some. But there is so much information out there, they get overwhelmed and quit.

Here is something else that made an impact on me. There are children who are frustrated by their parents as much as their parents are frustrated by them. Frustrated children will seek ways of coping. Many will experiment with drugs and alcohol, premarital sex, gang involvement, crime, pornography, and other self-destructive and anti-social behavior if things don't change. If the world is going to be improved, it must start with the family.

While doing my research I discovered what I was hoping to find. I discovered there is a way to create an environment where children behave because they want to, not because they are forced to, where children and parents treat each other with respect and kindness, and children feel free to show their feelings and discuss their problems. I learned WHY children misbehave and how parents can use that knowledge to turn their misbehavior around. I learned simple principles that parents can apply that will decrease their children's desire to misbehavior and increase their desire to cooperate.

I wanted to share this valuable, life-changing information with parents everywhere, and decided to write a book. But I wanted my book to be different from all the other parenting books. I remembered back to the days when I was a frustrated young parent and looking for a good book on parenting. There were so many, it was confusing. Did they all teach the same thing or were they all different? If they all taught the same thing, then why were there so many? If they were all different, then which one was the best?

I decided I would write a book that would contain the best parts out of the best books. I studied what some of the best experts had to say about raising children. I combed through thousands of pages of parenting books so parents wouldn't have to – over 40 books. I selected what I considered to be the essential information all parents need to know – information that just felt right to me. I simplified the information to make it easy to understand and easy to do. I condensed the information into a short book that takes only a couple of hours to read, and then made it available to parents everywhere. This is that one book I wish I had when I was a young parent.

This book comes with four promises:

1. **The book works.** I think you'll find that no matter where your children are on the behavior scale, applying the principles in this book will make things better.

2. **The book is short and to the point.** I've taken years of research and have condensed it all down into one short book to save you time. I've done the research so you don't have to.

3. **The book is easy to understand.** I've taken a complicated subject and simplified it so that anyone can understand it.

4. **The book is easy to do.** The suggestions I give are broken down into easy steps that anyone can follow.

I have written this book for anyone who spends time with children:

1. **For parents** – You have a challenging job that is 24 hours a day with little time off. This book promises to provide you with principles and skills that will engage cooperation among your children, preserve your sanity, and bring more joy into your life.

2. **For grandparents** – The quality of time you spend with your grandchildren will be enhanced by the principles and skills you learn and put into practice.

3. **For babysitters** – You will have the skills to combat problem behavior, which will make your job more enjoyable and make you a popular babysitter.

4. **For teachers** – The applications of principles and skills taught here will improve your ability to reach children and make a difference in their lives – and yours.

So who am I to be giving advice on raising kids? I'm a father of six children on which I have experimented with screaming, bribing, threatening, punishing, begging, giving in, and all forms of persuasion. I also discovered how to inspire good behavior by finding and applying principles that worked. The answers were out there, but not all in one place. My wife and I read books, attended seminars, listened to tapes, and received solicited and unsolicited advice from friends and family about kid behavior. I've made many mistakes. But I've also been successful at improving behavior. I know now how to do it and I want to share what I've learned with parents who are where I used to be: confused, frustrated and wanting to learn how to make life better. Now there is no reason that parents should have to think, "This isn't what I signed up for."

In this book I will introduce six steps that will dramatically improve child behavior. I refer to them as **"principles"**. By applying these principles, we can greatly raise the probability that good behavior will increase and unwanted behavior will go away. Children are "wired" to respond in predictable ways to what we say and do. Our children's good (and bad) behavior can be predicted by our words and actions.

Here are the six principles that are going to change your life. I call them The Incredibly Powerful and Effective Six Principles for Raising Happy Cooperative Kids and Making Parenthood a Joyful Experience. We can just call them The 6 Principles for short.

1. **Reward good behavior.** The behavior that gets the most attention is the behavior that will happen the most.

2. **Ignore annoying behavior.** These behaviors include complaining, whining, arguing and tantrums. The annoying behavior that receives no attention is the behavior that goes away.

3. **Spend personal time with each child.** This is quality, one-on-one time on a regular basis.

4. **Acknowledge Negative Feelings.** Learn how to listen and respond to your children to help them "let go" of their anger and negative feelings.

5. **Teach life skills.** This includes teaching children how to behave appropriately.

6. **Have weekly family meetings.** Spend time together as a family on a weekly basis.

When parents apply these principles, there is a mutual respect that forms between parents and their children. By applying these principles, parents show respect for their children. Children who feel respected *by* their parents develop more respect *for* their parents. They don't like to let their parents down. They feel more like cooperating. If you want to get respect from your kids, first you've got to give it. These principles will help you to do that. They will also improve your relationship with your children.

These 6 Principles can be applied to children of all ages, from toddlers to teens. Some specific parts of these principles are age specific and better applied to children than to teens. I've tried to make those parts obvious. And as I'm sure you are aware, misbehaviors come in various degrees, from not-so-bad to I-can't-take-it-anymore. I think you'll find that no matter where your child is on the behavior scale, applying The 6 Principles will make things better.

After I have introduced The 6 Principles, I will address **"techniques"** that you will use to deal directly with misbehaviors. The difference between a principle and a technique is that a principle is used to *decrease children's desire to misbehave and increase their desire to cooperate.* But since kids will be kids, misbehavior will always be an issue to some degree. That's where techniques come in. A technique is a skill that you will use to *respond to an unwanted behavior.* Some techniques will feel more comfortable than others. Use the ones that work best for you.

You cannot develop as much mutual respect with techniques as you can with The 6 Principles. The more principles you apply, and the longer you apply them, the better the techniques will work.

Both principles and techniques are "tools" for parents to use to improve their parenting skills. And just like any tool, principles and techniques take practice and patience to master. Don't hesitate to use these tools just because they are unfamiliar. You will experience success even if these tools feel awkward at first.

You Shouldn't Have to Go it Alone

I do not want you to feel alone while learning these principles and techniques. My hope is that you will get together with another parent (friend or neighbor) for mutual support. In this "support group" you will be able to talk about what you've read, bounce ideas back and forth, and share experiences. This support group need only start with you and someone you know. I believe that as you begin to experience the benefits of applying these principles and techniques, you will want to include other parents in your support group to talk about how love, common sense, and natural instincts are not enough. Parents need skills!

There is an African proverb that says: "It takes a village to raise a child". Wouldn't it give you comfort to know that when you send your children to school or to a neighbor's home, or use a babysitter, or visit grandma and grandpa, that those teachers, parents, babysitters and grandparents were aware of, and even practicing, the same principles and techniques that you are?

When parents become parents, they will find it natural to raise their children like they were raised. So the way you raise your children will probably be the way your children raise your grandchildren. Just think. In only two generations, the entire world will have a different generation of people making decisions that will have an effect on the world. The way they were raised and the relationship they have with their parents will be a basis on which they will make decisions. The way we raise our children today really can make a difference in how the world will look tomorrow.

Parenting is a tough job. I don't pretend that this book will make raising kids easy, or that it will make parenting enjoyable all the time, but I feel confident in making this promise: *If you do what this book teaches, things will improve.* Things will get better. You will catch your children doing and saying things that will make you smile and warm your heart more often. At the end of the day, you will look back on it and realize that in spite of all the problems, drama and chaos, the small moments of joy will have made your day a good one.

As parents, we are all in this raising-kids-thing together. This book is my contribution. It is my hope that it gives you the answers you've been looking for. So let's get started. I've done the hard part. I've learned what works and what doesn't. Now sit back. Watch and learn. I'll teach you the skills. You take what you learn and put into practice. Take a deep breath. Your world is about to change. Here we go.

Chapter 2 - Why Children Misbehave

As a parent, sometimes you'll tell your children NOT to do something, and they'll do it anyway. Sometimes you'll tell your children to do something, and they won't do it.

Sometimes you'll hear someone knocking at the front door who turns out to be the two-year-old who only moments ago was safely in the backyard, or so you thought, and then he will point to his four-year-old brother who has climbed the neighbor's tree and won't come down.

Sometimes it will get real quiet and you can't find the children because they've hidden themselves somewhere in the house – or at least you hope they're still in the house – and you want to strangle the person who said parenting will come naturally.

Experiences like these made me want to do one of two things: either have nothing more to do with little kids – EVER, or, figure them out. I chose to figure them out. And I'm glad I did.

I want to teach you something I learned that caused me to see children in a whole new light. What I learned was nothing less than fascinating. I learned why children misbehave. And then I learned things I could do to take away their desire to behave badly and give them a desire to cooperate. Raising children went from frustrating to interesting to enjoyable. Now I want you to have the same experience. So let's start with the foundation on which everything will be built: why children misbehave.

The Two Built-in Needs of Every Child

Children are always trying to achieve two things: 1) **belonging** and 2) **personal power**. It's wired into their brains although they are not consciously aware of it. They can't help but seek after a sense of belonging and personal power. It's what they were born to do. It is one thing you can always count on. Knowing this can be very helpful.

Belonging

Every child needs to feel a sense of belonging. Children crave to feel needed, valued, and recognized as a part of the family. To a child, belonging means to feel noticed, included, accepted and loved. A child craves for his parent's attention and approval. When a child does not feel a sense of belonging, he feels ignored, left out, forgotten, rejected. And a child cannot bear to feel that way. So even though a child doesn't consciously realize it, he is constantly looking for ways to feel like he belongs.

If a child does not feel a sense of belonging, he will go after it on his own. Every hour of every day he will explore methods (or behaviors) to give him a sense of belonging. And when he discovers a behavior that brings him that good feeling, he will repeat that behavior. If his behavior does not result in a feeling of belonging, he will abandon that behavior. After all, what good is a behavior if it doesn't meet his need? He learns by trial and error.

Personal Power

Feeling a sense of personal power is the second need that motivates a child's behavior. Where a sense of belonging means to feel included, a sense of personal power means to feel significant, in charge of oneself, having the freedom to choose, to feel empowered. Children have a keen sense of observation. They observe that mom and dad have all the power – the power to command what to eat, when to eat, when to go to bed, when to get up, what to wear, what to do, what not to do. Children decide early in their lives that they want to feel power too. It happens to all children. It's a basic need. It's how they start to become independent, and after all, ultimately, isn't that what we want them to become: independent, able to think for themselves, take care of themselves, make decisions and be accountable for their actions? That starts with personal power. The need for personal power is wired into every child.

If a child does not feel a sense of personal power, she will go after it, and the easiest way to feel personal power is to simply say "no" to a request or "command" from a parent. When she discovers that refusing to obey brings a feeling of personal power, she will repeat that behavior. Choosing to obey is the one thing she has complete control over no matter what her age.

How Children Meet their Own Needs

Children start out life knowing nothing. They learn through observing, exploring and experimenting. They are like little scientists, always experimenting. From their failures they draw the conclusion: "Hmmm. This didn't meet my needs. Make a mental note to avoid doing it in the future." From their successes they draw the conclusion: "Ah! This is how I can belong. This is how I can feel personal power. If it worked once, it should work again." Their successful experiments and repeated actions are what we call behavior.

Children have undeveloped minds. That's a good thing because we can have a big influence on how those minds are developed. But that can be a bad thing because left on their own, children make mistaken conclusions from their experiments.

For example, a child might conclude that hitting, teasing, throwing tantrums, whining and getting into mischief is a good way to get mom or dad's attention, and getting their attention gives him a sense of belonging. Children learn that although these behaviors bring an angry reaction from parents, it is better than no reaction at all.

A child might conclude that arguing, ignoring parents and being defiant builds his sense of personal power. Imagine what power a child must feel knowing he can make mom and dad angry anytime he wants. He learns how to push their buttons. He takes pleasure in teasing his sibling in order to get a predictable angry or negative reaction from his parents.

Now that we know the two basic needs that every child has (the need to feel a sense of belonging and personal power) we can do things, as parents, to meet those needs in positive ways which will result in good behavior. Children don't care HOW those needs are met, only that they ARE met. Granted, they will still explore, experiment, create, make mistakes, get into trouble, and have as much fun as they can. That's how kids learn and grow. But once those basic needs are met, there's really no reason for children to try to meet those needs on their own by repeatedly misbehaving.

Children misbehave when they are left on their own to figure out how to meet their two built-in needs. Children behave "good" when their parents, caregivers, babysitters and teachers have helped them meet their two built-in needs in positive ways.

We've learned that misbehavior is not random. Your child is on a mission to feel a sense of belonging and personal power. All the arguing, interrupting, whining, talking back, ignoring and other misbehaviors are symptoms of a deeper issue. If we focus only on the bad behavior by yelling, spanking, reminding, nagging and punishing, the bad behavior might go away for a while, but it will return. However, if we focus on the deeper issue, helping our children meet their two basic needs in positive ways, the bad behavior will go away and stay away.

The 6 Principles that you are about to learn will help you meet your children's two basic needs in positive ways, and as a result, their behavior will improve.

Chapter 3 - What Doesn't Work

A lady was shopping at a grocery store and couldn't help but notice a young mother and her little girl who was about two years old. The little girl was crying loudly as she sat in the child seat in the shopping cart, but the mother seemed remarkably composed under the pressure. As the lady passed the mother in the aisle, she heard the mother calmly say, "It's okay, Emma, we're going to be out of here pretty soon and then we can go home."

The little girl's crying did not stop. When the lady passed the mother in another aisle, she heard the mother say, "Calm down Emma. We're almost done and then we can go."

As luck would have it, the lady found herself behind the mother at the checkout stand, her child still screaming. She overheard the mother say, "Look Emma, all we have to do is pay for our groceries and we're out of here?"

The lady, impressed with the mother's self-control, couldn't help but comment to the mother, "I must say, I am impressed at how well you are handling your daughter Emma's tantrum." "Oh, thank you," said the mother, "But my daughter's name is Ashley. I'm Emma."

Out with the Old

This little story reminds me of the many times I've seen children misbehave at the supermarket and other public places and have observed how parents handle the situation. It also reminds me of how I used to handle similar situations. I discovered that if I got mad and made a threat (do it or else), my children would obey. "If you don't get over here right now and sit down, I'm going to paddle your behind." I got the result I wanted immediately. So I figured because it worked, that must be the way to do it. When I found my kids were slow to obey, I would just raise my voice and repeat. Sometimes I had to get angry and scream. Now, that got their attention, but I started to notice that asking and demanding weren't working so well anymore, and I was compelled to scream more often to get my kids to obey. I later learned that my method of discipline was called coercion. I was trying to "make" my kids obey. I've since learned that even though coercion produces short-term compliance, it does not result in long-term cooperation.

Oh, I used other techniques, alright. I used them often to coerce, or make, my kids do what I wanted. I would say things like:

"I'm so sick and tired of you acting like this."

"You're driving me crazy."

"Aren't you ever going to learn to behave?"

"I'm going to count to three…"

"If you do that one more time, I'm going to put you in timeout!"

"If you do that one more time, I'm going to put you in timeout – and I mean it this time!"

"And while you're in timeout, think about what you did!"

I spoke from a deep feeling of frustration, not knowing what to do. I would scold, scream, spank, threaten and lecture. My children got very good at tuning out my lectures but appearing like they were listening. My lectures would include phrases that I thought were behavior-changing like:

"Why did you hit your sister?"

"How many times am I going to have to tell you to quit hitting?"

"Do you like it when someone hits you?"

And how about this pearl of wisdom: "Who said life was fair?"

I started to observe other families and how other parents related with their children. I noticed that in families where the parents used the coercion-style of discipline, some of their children would grow up to use coping behaviors that included drugs, alcohol, tobacco, pornography, sex, failing school, and getting into trouble with the law. Some even had issues with suicide. I've since learned that many kids use coping behaviors like these just to get even with their parents. I did not want this to be the fate of any of my children. I had dreams for my kids. I wanted them to grow up happy, learn life-skills, and become successful adults. Not only that, my wife and I were tired of the constant pounding we took as we tried to get our kids to do what we asked.

Out of desperation I sought advice: I read books, experimented with discipline techniques, and eventually came up with a new set of methods to replace the old set that didn't work. Now, when I watch other parents handle misbehavior with the same methods that I used to use, I want to tap them on the shoulder and say, "Excuse me. There's a better way!"

So I'm going to ask you to examine your methods; take the old methods that don't work like screaming, threatening, criticizing, using sarcasm, arguing and punishing, and replace them with new methods that do work; methods that I know you will be much happier with.

Strict vs. Permissive

There are two common discipline styles used among parents. They are commonly called "strict" and "permissive".

Some parents are strict and controlling when it comes to raising their children. They make demands and they lecture. They lay down the law, and children who don't obey the law face punishment. They tell their children, "You do it because I said so."

Children who are raised in a strict environment tend to be rebellious, if not in the presence of their parents, then secretively behind their backs. They become excellent liars. They are irresponsible. They blame other people or circumstances for their bad behavior rather than taking responsibility themselves. Their sense of personal power might come from bullying others. Still, other children in a strict environment may become fearfully submissive. Many parents who discipline with strictness and punishment have a hard time giving up their style because of the mistaken belief that the only alternative is permissiveness.

Then there are other parents who are very permissive and lenient when it comes to raising their children. They prefer to avoid confrontation and as a result, their children "walk all over them". They might make rules, only to allow their children to break them without any consequences.

Children who are raised in a permissive environment develop an entitlement attitude. They form the belief that others should take care of them. They manipulate mom and dad into taking care of their every wish through whining, tantrums and arguing. They mistakenly believe that to feel valued they must have constant attention, and misbehaving is the only way they know how to get that attention.

Neither strict nor permissive environments help meet children's most basic needs: a sense of belonging and a sense of personal power, and when those needs are not adequately met, misbehavior will surely result.

There is a third style of discipline which we will focus on here. It goes by various names: Positive Discipline, Positive Parenting, but it all boils down to using firmness with dignity and respect. It involves making rules and allowing consequences to happen. It involves teaching problem-solving and giving choices. It does not involve excessive control or permissiveness, but does involve learning to listen and allowing children to learn from their mistakes.

Children are used to getting certain responses from parents. When we change our responses, they might exaggerate their behavior (get worse) in an effort to get us to respond like they are used to seeing. So be prepared, and take comfort in knowing that it is a normal response and shouldn't last very long.

Say Goodbye to Screaming

I used to be a screamer. I remember saying to my children on many occasions, "I'm sorry I screamed. But it was the only way I could get you to listen!" When you learn the principles I'm about to show you, you will no longer find it necessary to scream. And when you don't have to scream, you'll feel better about yourself. You'll feel less guilt, less stress, and more peace.

Your children will also do better. Screaming does not promote a feeling of belonging. Although it might give a child the attentions that he seeks after, it's a negative kind of attention and promotes misbehavior. Screaming can also lead to a power struggle between you and your child.

So, screaming is one of the techniques that you are going to get rid of. It will be replaced by a new technique called Your Calm Voice. Use Your Calm Voice anytime you're around your children. See if this one technique doesn't make a positive difference in your whole family.

The Problem with Asking "Why" Questions

"Why didn't you come when I called?" "Why did you hit your brother?" "Why didn't you do your homework?" Asking "why" questions never helps improve behavior. When you ask your child to explain her behavior, are you really looking for an answer, or are you just blowing off steam? Asking "why" questions focuses on the bad behavior, and when attention is given to bad behavior, that behavior is reinforced and strengthened. "Why" questions also encourage blaming. "Well, he hit me first." We will look at much better ways to improve behavior. In the meantime, steer away from asking "why" questions.

The Child is not the Behavior

The child is not the behavior. In other words, behavior is separate from the child. If the behavior is bad, that does not mean the child is bad.

Just like pain is the symptom of a cavity, behavior is the symptom of a deeper issue. You can temporarily reduce the pain of a cavity with pain pills. But that will not fix what's causing the pain. You can focus on your child's bad behavior but that will not fix the problem causing the bad behavior. Only when you focus on the root cause of bad behavior will you be able to change the behavior in the long run.

Behavior is a window into what motivates a child to behave the way he or she does. After you learn the principles that this book teaches, you will be able to observe the behavior of your children and determine if it is caused by a need for a sense of belonging or a need for a feeling of personal power. Then, you will be able to focus on the cause and watch the behavior change. That doesn't mean that bad behavior shouldn't be addressed. It should be. So we will also be working on effective ways to manage bad behavior at the same time we are working on its cause. We will look at both fixing the cause and treating the symptoms.

Why Punishment Doesn't Work

Try this little experiment: ask some parents you know, "What motivates children to obey rules?" You'll get various answers but I think the most common answer will be: "Because they're afraid of what will happen if they don't." I learned that the threat of punishment is a good motivator in the short run, but has bad consequences in the long run.

Throughout this book I try to drive home the point that the first thing parents need to do to change bad behavior into good behavior is to help the child meet two powerful, built-in needs: 1) feel a sense of belonging, and 2) feel a sense of personal power. Punishment does not help the child meet either of these needs in positive ways and that is why punishment does not result in long-term good behavior.

5-year-old Amelia and her brother were teasing each other during dinner. As Amelia went to block her brother's attempt to touch her plate, she knocked over her glass of water filling her plate and spilling onto the table. A common parental reaction would be to make her misbehavior feel so unpleasant that she will think twice before ever attempting to repeat her wrongdoing. In other words, she must "pay" for her mistake. She might be banished from the table, spanked, scolded, or forced to eat her remaining soggy food.

The problem with this method of discipline is that instead of learning from her mistake, Amelia will focus on feeling rejected, which is the opposite of feeling a sense of belonging. Punishment encourages children to blame someone else for their own misdeed: "He made me do it!" Punishment also promotes lying. Why would Amelia ever want to tell the truth if she knew it would lead to punishment?

There are basically three reasons people punish their kids.

1. It works – in the short term. Punishment will stop the misbehavior immediately.

2. Parents feel that letting a child get away with a bad behavior will encourage the child to repeat the offense. So, rather than coming across as permissive, it is better to show disapproval by punishing.

3. Parents don't know what else to do. Applying punishment seems to be the only option available.

Jane Nelsen, Ed.D., in her book *Positive Discipline*[1], says, "Where did we ever get the crazy idea that in order to make children do better, first we have to make them feel worse? Think of the last time you felt humiliated or were treated unfairly. Did you feel like cooperating or doing better?"

I believe that if we are to create peace in the world, we must first create peace in the home. Punishment does not create peace in the home.

Punishment gives younger children negative attention. And for children who lack a strong sense of belonging, negative attention is better than no attention at all. So, even though punishment stops misbehavior immediately, the misbehavior will happen again and again.

Punishment doesn't work with older children because it causes them to seek revenge or think about how they are going to avoid getting caught next time.

Words Have Power

Words have the power to change behavior. If you want to change behavior, change your words. Here is how it works. Parent's words have an impact on how their children feel. Children's feelings have an impact on what they think. What they think leads to what they do (or how they behave).

Parent's words → how children feel → what children think → how children behave

Change your words and the behavior changes. That means not only to say the right thing at the right time, but to be aware of what not to say and when it's best to say nothing at all. This book teaches you to be mindful of what you say, and realize that what you say really matters.

A father and his son are throwing the Frisbee in the backyard. The son makes a wild throw and the Frisbee lands on the roof of the house. The father has a choice. He can say, "That wasn't a very smart thing to do," or he could say, "Opps," in a lighthearted way. Each response will result in the son feeling a different way.

This book will give you the opportunity to choose your response with an understanding of the feeling it will cause.

Now it's time to introduce you to the 6 Principles.

Section 1 - Appling Principles

Decrease Children's Desire to Misbehave and Increase their Desire to Cooperate

Chapter 4 - Principle #1 - Reward Good Behavior

I will introduce this principle by directing your attention to the following statement. Please read it carefully because it is the foundation of this principle; the reason it works.

The behavior that receives the most attention is the behavior that will happen the most.

Will you agree with me, that most of the time, the behavior that receives the most attention is the bad behavior? Well, if the above statement is true, and I'm claiming it is, then the following statement must also be true.

If you pay attention to good behavior, it will happen more often.

Child psychologists say this is one of the best ways to change bad behavior to good behavior. I've seen it work and I know parents who were amazed at how quickly their children's behavior changed when they applied this principle. Here is what you do:

Look for good behavior and reward it.

Rewarding good behavior does not mean bribing or giving gifts or treats for good behavior. It means giving positive attention to good behavior. It means watching each of the children, and when one of them behaves in a good way, rewarding him or her with a kind word, compliment or action. Here are some examples:

Walk past two children who are coloring and say, "You children are playing together so nicely."

A child is playing quietly with blocks. You say, "You are so good to play quietly." Then touch him on his shoulder as you walk by.

A child is eating. You say, "You are getting better at using your spoon", and give her a big smile.

Reward children with a kind word when they are in a good mood, playing together nicely, doing what you asked, getting their homework done, not causing trouble, and generally behaving well. This makes children want to behave because *the behavior that receives the most attention, is the behavior that will happen the most.*

If you give good behavior more attention, good behavior will happen more often. Here is the challenge. Usually when children are behaving well, it's easy to ignore them. "Leave well enough alone," you might say. Don't ignore them! Watch for opportunities to reward good behavior.

Even children who are *always* misbehaving will accidently do something right. You might say, "I noticed you walked past your brother without teasing him". (You're thinking: Even if you were clear across the room and didn't even notice him). "Thank you."

The more positive attention you give a child who exhibits good behavior, the more you will reinforce that behavior. The more positive attention you give a child who exhibits bad behavior, the more you will motivate that child to change his behavior. You have to watch for opportunities. Sometimes you have to watch really hard.

Imagine a child who gets many rewards a day. The positive attention is starting to feel good. He wants more. It feels good to behave "good". The positive attention is directly fulfilling his need to belong. He's being noticed. He feels accepted by receiving your attention without having to misbehave to get it. Why misbehave to get attention when it feels so good to behave? Children who are not used to being rewarded for good behavior will thrive on the shower of rewards you give them. They will behave well because they like receiving your unsolicited attention and approval.

Dr. Glenn I. Latham, in his book, *The Power of Positive Parenting[1]*, states: "Research has shown that the most effective way to reduce problem behavior in children is to strengthen desirable behavior through positive reinforcement rather than trying to weaken undesirable behavior using aversive or negative processes." Dr. Latham feels this statement is so important, that he includes it at the end of every chapter.

How many rewards is enough? Reward each child several times an hour if you can. For children who misbehave often, give more, maybe 12 rewards per hour. That's one every 5 minutes. For children who misbehave less often, it may not be necessary to give so many, but keep this in mind. If your good-behaving children see you giving more rewards to your misbehaving children than they are getting, they will conclude that to get more of your attention, they should misbehave more. To keep that from happening, distribute rewards evenly and sincerely among all of your children. Kids from toddlers to teens thrive on positive rewards. As children grow into their teenage years, you may find it harder to give them rewards. However, they still need them, so try to give them some every day.

If you are watching more than one child, then you have your work cut out for you. But the result will be worth it and you will be glad you made the effort. If this seems overwhelming, just do the best you can. After a while it will seem so natural that you will notice good behavior and reward it without even thinking about it.

You can also reward good behavior later, upon hearing about it. Dad might say, "Mom said you put on your shoes the first time you were asked. Nice going."

Don't make a big deal out of giving positive attention. Just two or three seconds is all it takes. Don't let too much time go by without catching each child doing something right, and rewarding each child with kind words or actions. Below is a list of ideas to say or do. You will think of more depending on the situation. Use them liberally, when you see the opportunity.

Positive things to say:
Good thinking.
You're really using your head.
Good idea.
You did it!
Nice going. Gimme five.
I couldn't have done it better myself.
I couldn't have done it without you.
You and I, we make a good team.

I had no idea you colored so well.
You're getting better at staying inside the lines.
I didn't know you could read so well.
This is good work.
You guys are playing together so nicely.
Hey, that's pretty good.
Hey, that's a great improvement.
Good job.
You're getting better.
That's neat.
You make it look easy.
Thank you.
I'm proud of you for...
You didn't quit.
You're doing a great job.
You did a good job at…
I really appreciate you being such a good helper.
You should be proud of yourself.
I see you've decided to share your toys. Good for you.
You are helping your sister draw. That's great.
This looks great. You must have worked hard at it.
That was a really good try.
I love to see you smile.
I love listening to you play the piano.

Anything that starts with "I notice..."
I notice you are sitting quietly.
I noticed you were nice to your sister all morning.
I've noticed that you've really been in control.

Anything that starts with "I like..."
I like the way you are sharing.
I like how you did that.

I like that idea.

I like the colors you chose.

I like it when you chew with your mouth shut.

I like how you did that the first time I asked.

Anything that starts with "I'm impressed..."

I'm impressed with how nice your room looks.

I'm impressed that you didn't hit your sister back.

I'm impressed how you took care of the baby.

Anything that begins with "Thank you..."

Thank you for doing that without an argument.

Thanks for doing what I asked.

Thank you for doing that without being asked.

Positive things to do:

a hug

a pat on the back

a high-five

a low-five

a touch on the shoulder

a soft punch on the arm

a fist bump

a smile

a thumbs-up

a note left for them to find

a card they receive in the mail from you

a laugh (with them, not at them)

a wink

a wave

a touch on the arm

Paul Axtell, in his book, *Ten Powerful Things to Say to Your Kids*[2], says, "Your words have the power to create. What are you creating for your child with your words? If you see something in your child and you acknowledge it, that characteristic will continue to develop and grow. Whether it's positive or negative, whatever you pay attention to grows. So choose the good things to focus on."

When you reward good behavior, make sure your rewards are sincere, evenly given to all the children, and done frequently. The smaller the child, the more enthusiastic you should be. When you use this skill, your children will show good behavior more often and unwanted behavior less often.

Another way to reward good behavior is to write a note: "I noticed you shared your crayons with your brother this morning. That made me smile." Slip the note in his lunchbox, coat pocket, inside his book cover, anywhere he will find it.

Piggyback a Value

Occasionally, piggyback a reward with an enduring value. First, reward the good behavior. "Wow! You cleaned both bathrooms." Then tack on a value statement: "That was very ambitious of you. "Ambitious" is the value. By adding on a value statement, you reinforce the value, and that encourages the child to repeat it. Here is the structure of the entire statement:

Thank you for _____. That was very _____.

Here are some examples:

Thank you for telling the truth. That was very honest of you.

Thank you for rocking the baby to sleep. That was very helpful of you.

Thank you for sharing your toy. That was very unselfish of you.

Thank you for not hitting your sister back. That showed a lot of self-control.

Thank you for doing your chores every day last week. That shows you are dependable.

Other values include:

Courageous	Generous
Forgiving	Loving
Polite	Responsible
Kind	Respectful
Fast learner	Hard worker

Try a little experiment. Choose one negative behavior you'd like to see your child change. Decide what the opposite behavior would be. For example, the opposite of not getting into bed when asked is getting into bed when asked. The opposite of teasing your little brother is not teasing your little brother. Then watch for a small glimmer of opposite (positive) behavior and reward it when you see it. "I only had to ask you to get into bed three times tonight instead of the usual four. That's an improvement. Thank you." Or, "I noticed you played nicely with your bother for almost 10 minutes. High five."

I think you'll find that after children have been rewarded for good behavior for a while, just the anticipation of receiving another reward will influence how they behave.

Giving compliments is not reserved only for kids. Parents should use compliments on each other to show appreciation. If you want to reinforce or change your spouse's behavior, look for good behavior and reward it.

No More Criticizing

The first principle Dale Carnegie teaches in his timeless book, *How To Win Friends & Influence People*[3], is to stop using criticism as a means to change people. Although he is speaking about people in general, it applies to parents. He writes, "Criticism is futile because it puts a person on the defensive and usually makes him strive to justify himself. Criticism is dangerous, because it wounds a person's precious pride, hurts his sense of importance, and arouses resentment."

Whenever I hear a successful athlete being interviewed, he or she will give the reason for achieving great success by saying something like, "The coach always gave me praise and encouragement and that motivated me to be the best I could." You will *never* hear an athlete say, "The coach criticized me all the time and that motivated me to do the best I could."

Think of the last time you were criticized. Did it motivate you to strive to do better, or did it hurt your feelings. Did is cause you to want to improve, or did it cause resentment. Children are no different. Criticism does not motivate children to improve their behavior. It does not create a desire to cooperate. Criticism contributes to misbehavior.

Chapter 5 - Principle #2 - Ignore Annoying Behavior

Many of the things kids do that drive parents crazy should not be given any attention at all. Just turn and walk away. Just ignore it.

If the behavior that receives the most attention is the behavior that will happen the most (as explained in the previous chapter), then the opposite must also be true:

The behavior that does not get any attention is the behavior that will go away.

If you pay attention to annoying behavior, it will likely continue. If you ignore annoying behavior, it will likely stop. When kids argue and tease one another, just walk out of the room. Much of the time they are simply performing for an audience: you! And if you pay attention to them, it encourages their performance.

When kids are showing annoying behavior, it's a normal reaction for you to want to scream, "Stop that right now!" Try not to do that. Instead, pretend it's not happening. Remember that annoying behaviors are usually just normal, growing-up behaviors. Some kids do annoying things just to see if they can get a reaction out of the parent. Don't get caught in their trap.

Pay no attention to annoying behavior, don't look at it, comment about it, roll your eyes or shake your head. Leave the room if you must. Ignoring annoying behavior works best after you have been rewarding the children for good behavior. So after the children have experienced being rewarded for good behavior, then start ignoring annoying behavior.

You have to decide whether the behavior should be ignored or not. Behaviors that should be ignored are those behaviors that bug us, annoy us, and frustrate us. They can be throwing a tantrum, whining, pleading, crying, teasing, being loud, complaining, arguing, and so on. As long as no one is getting hurt (physically or emotionally) and no property is in danger of being damaged, feel free to ignore. As simple as this sounds, it is difficult for most parents to do because it runs contrary to how we normally respond to such occurrences.

You ask your child to vacuum the carpet. "Why should I have to vacuum all the time?" he complains. "There are other people here. They make just as much mess as I do. Why don't they have to vacuum? I'm sick and tire of always being asked to do stuff. I've got a life too, you know."

If you want to encourage this kind of annoying behavior, just jump into the argument. "It will take you all of 10 minutes to vacuum. Why don't we change jobs? I'll do what you do and you do what I do? Think that would make you happier? I know it would me!" As much as you are tempted to respond with something like that, don't respond. Just listen. Don't shake your head, roll your eyes, or show any reaction. Then when he or she is done ranting, you can say, "I'm not going to argue about it." Once the chore is done, give a reward: "That sure looks better. Thank you." You'll get a response like, "Whatever," which you will ignore. Behaviors that get no attention are behaviors that dry up and blow away.

You say to your child, "I'd like you to be home by nine o'clock. Now, what time did I tell you to be home by?" You might get this: "Nine o'clock?! Why so early? Can't I stay 'till ten? Even nine thirty? I'm not a baby, you know. Why do you treat me like a baby?" to which you listen with no reaction, and then respond with, "That's exactly right. Nine o'clock. Thank you." No arguing, no fighting, just a lot of ignoring.

Now when you first try this, kids might test you. They might increase the annoying behavior just to see what you will do. But once they figure out that you are serious, the annoying behavior should go away. Then reward the child for not being annoying: "I noticed you haven't teased your bother" (in the last 3 minutes.) Then give a thumbs-up. Then later, "I noticed you haven't teased your bother". (in the last 20 minutes.) Then smile. Here are some other things you might say:

You've been good to stay off the table.

I see your shoes are still on. Good going.

That was a good job asking without whining.

I love it when you talk instead of cry.

I noticed you *asked* your sister for her toy. Nice going. Give me five.

I like it when you talk softly.

Thank you for sharing.

Give an Ignore Warning

You may want to try warning your child that the next time he does something worthy of ignoring, you are going to ignore him. That way the child will know what you are doing. For example, when you are not on the phone, you could say, "Sit down here, I have something to tell you. You know how I'm on the phone sometimes and you have a question and can't wait for me to finish my phone call? Well, from now on, I want you to wait. In fact, if you whine or bug me while I'm on the phone, I'm just going to ignore you. It's not that I don't care, I do. And I'll be glad to help you after I'm done with my phone call. So, just so I know you understand, if you want me to talk to you while I'm on the phone, what will I do? That's exactly right. I will ignore you."

Let's say that you have a child who throws tantrums. While your child is calm, you could say, "Honey, I want to tell you something. You know how sometimes when you want something and I tell you 'No', and you feel mad and scream and cry and kick your legs? Well, from now on, when you do that, I'm going to ignore you. That means I will pretend that you are not there. It's not that I don't care, I do. And I'll be glad to talk with you after you're feeling better. So, next time you get mad and scream and cry and kick your legs, what am I going to do? That's right. I will ignore you. But I will still love you."

In these two examples, we have set expectations in somewhat of a formal manner. We could have said, "Next time you interrupt me while I'm on the phone...," or "Next time you throw a tantrum, I'm going to ignore you." That is more of an informal way. The informal way is quick and to the point, but does not make as much of an impression on kids as the formal way. For more information on setting expectations, see chapter 10, Making Rules.

Now this is important. If you noticed your child waiting for your phone call to end, or you notice an abnormally short tantrum, be sure to reward the good behavior. "I noticed you waited for me to get done with my phone call. That was great. Okay, what did you need?" Or, "I noticed that you controlled yourself better. Do you want to talk?"

Here is a quick review:

1. If you pay attention to a good behavior, it will happen more often. (this is a good thing)

2. If you pay attention to an annoying behavior, *it* will happen more often. (this is a bad thing)

3. If you ignore an annoying behavior, it will go away. (this is a good thing)

4. If you ignore a good behavior, *it* will go away. (this is a bad thing)

Chapter 6 - Principle #3 - Spend Personal Time with Each Child

Spending personal time with each child communicates that you value them and consider them to be an important part of the family. Using this principle is one of the best ways to help each child meet their need to feel a sense of belonging. It gives them what they most desperately want from you: your complete attention. If they can get that, their negative attention-getting behaviors disappear.

Spending personal time with each child also helps them satisfy their need to feel a sense of personal power. Personal power is the freedom to choose, and because you allow the child to choose the activity, you reduce the child's desire to meet that need in negative ways.

Let me put it another way. If you don't spend personal time with each child, you will end up spending more time dealing with their negative behaviors. Wouldn't you rather spend time preventing problems than fixing them? Wouldn't you rather spend time having a good time with each child rather than fighting with them?

You won't believe what a difference this principle will make in your child's behavior. Here's the principle in a little more detail:

Each parent spends uninterrupted time with each child, every day, doing what the child wants to do.

Here is the ideal way to use this principle:

1. Give the principle a more personal name, like, "Daddy Kaitlyn Time".

2. Do it every day if possible. Even 10 minutes a day is better than no minutes.

3. Give 100% of your attention to your child. No distractions. No siblings.

4. Let your child decide how your time is to be spent.

5. This is not a time to talk about their dirty room, chores not completed or other needed improvements.

6. Never threaten to cancel personal time as a way to improve behavior: "If you misbehave like that again, no Daddy Kaitlyn Time today." That is like saying, "If you continue to stay sick, I will stop giving you medicine."

Finding Time

Okay, let's get real. For some parents it's impossible to spend personal time with each child every day. If you can't do it every day, do it as often as you can. Just remember, the more often and regularly you can spend one-on-one time with each child, the better they will respond.

If you must postpone house cleaning, sacrifice Facebook time, cancel your cable or reschedule your workout to find personal time to spend with each child, the rewards will be worth it. If the family is a 2-parent family, ideally, both parents should spend time with each child daily.

Distractions

Sometimes distractions cannot be avoided. But keep in mind that one of the things that make this principle work so well is that you are satisfying your child's need for your total attention. Your child should not have to compete with anyone or anything. If you are mentally making a grocery list or talking on the phone and only half-focused on your child, your child will feel your insincere interest. If that happens, this principle will lose its effectiveness.

If you have other children, consider putting on a fun DVD to keep them busy, or getting someone to look after them. The other children, however, will be better behaved knowing that they just had, or will soon have their turn with you. And since you are always looking to reward good behavior, you might say, "I noticed you were quiet during the time I spent with your brother. Thank you."

Activities

Let your child decide how you are to spend your time together. You will be entering her world and doing what she likes to do, so be ready to play. Depending on her age, you might be building a tower with blocks, reading a book together, kicking around the soccer ball, or just talking. Your time together should be face to face. No TV. Be prepared to give your child a choice between two activities if she can't think one. "Would you like to play a game or read a book?"

Here is a list of some of the things that my wife and I have done with our children:

1. I remember lying next to each of my children in their bed at night and just talking.
2. We would lie on the trampoline at night with blankets and pillows and look at the stars. Occasionally we would see a shooting star or a satellite. If you don't have a tramp, the grass works just fine.
3. Play catch – some of my kids can throw a pretty good fastball. So can my wife.
4. Play a game – backgammon was a favorite of some of my children. We would also play the "matching" game with Old Maid cards – turn them all face down and take turns tuning over two cards, trying to find a matching pair.
5. Throw the Frisbee
6. Shoot some hoops
7. Read together
8. Take a trip to the library. Check out a book on "activities for children" and read it together. Choose an activity and do it. Find some good story books to check out as well.
9. Bake something together
10. Build something with blocks or Lego's
11. Draw or color something
12. Go to a golf course. Practice putting on the putting green, hit a bucket of balls, or play a round.
13. Build a snowman
14. Make snow angels
15. Have a picnic – outdoors or indoors

16. Visit a museum
17. Take the dog to a dog training class together
18. Walk the dog together or just take a walk together
19. Write a letter together to someone you both know – like grandma, or a friend
20. Look at family photos together
21. Sing songs
22. Tell stories about when your child was a toddler or a baby
23. Simply hold your child
24. Build a blanket fort
25. Plant flower or vegetable seeds. Tend it together – or plant a garden.
26. Go to a movie
27. Finger Paint
28. Take pictures or video – make a movie
29. Visit an aquarium
30. Put together a puzzle
31. Build a fire together – then make s'mores
32. Build something with wood – maybe a bird house
33. Make homemade pizza
34. Rake leaves and jump in the pile
35. Make water balloons. Play catch with one as you slowly back further away from each other.
36. Go on a bike ride
37. Find a fruit tree and pick fruit together – apples, apricots, pears, etc.
38. Play hide and seek
39. Paint fingernails and toenails together
40. Go on a hike

41. Attend a baseball, basketball, soccer, or football game
42. Go fishing
43. Go out for sundaes or ice cream cones
44. Go out for pie, bagels, donuts, pizza or burgers
45. Go for a ride on a train, bus, or subway
46. Go horseback riding
47. Go outside when it's raining (and warm) and get totally soaked together
48. Paint a picture by numbers together
49. Go to a theater or dance performance
50. Wash the car
51. Do dishes together
52. Clean out a closet together
53. Fly a kite
54. Jump rope
55. Exercise together
56. Write a story. Take turns writing only 3 or 4 words per turn.
57. Go bowling – or set up a bowling alley in your hall with empty 2-liter plastic bottles and a softball.
58. Play Simon Says
59. Play "I Spy"
60. Listen to music and play homemade instruments together
61. Start a journal with each child
62. Prepare a family meal together
63. Start a collection
64. Play with sidewalk chalk
65. Play tetherball
66. Play ping pong

67. Indoor golf (putters only)
68. Tell jokes
69. Play hillbilly golf (Google it)
70. Go jogging together – enter a 1 mile or 5K race
71. Attend an auction together
72. Visit a play ground

Young children might cry at the end of your personal time together, wanting to extend it. In this case you could have something planned for her to do. You might say, "Why don't you come into the kitchen and help me with dinner?" Or, "Why don't you come into the kitchen and color while I get dinner ready?" Once you get into the routine, this should become less of an issue.

Here are some situations to avoid because they might motivate bad behavior:

1. You spend personal time with one child but not with another.

2. You spend noticeably more time with one child than with another.

3. You cancel personal time when the child is looking forward to it.

Eat Together as a Family

Studies have shown that when families regularly eat together, and the conversation is positive, children are more likely to exhibit good behavior. Eating family dinner together is a good way to share values and bond with family members.

Remember to look for good behavior and reward it. Compliment children on their good table manners. "I notice that you're chewing your food with your mouth closed. I like that. Thank you." Keep criticism away from family meals as much as possible. If certain table manners need to be improved on, those manners should be taught or revisited at another time (if it's not too obnoxious). See chapter 8 on teaching life skills.

Pleasant conversation at family meal time will promote family bonding, and can be a good way to learn about what your kids are doing and thinking. A good way to get people talking is to ask a question for everyone to answer. "So, tell us one good thing that happened to you today." Questions get people thinking, and interesting conversations can result. Go around the table and give everyone a chance to respond. Remember, no criticizing, lecturing or arguing. Just listen and try to understand. Here is a list of possible subjects to get you started.

"What is one good thing that happened to you today?"

"If you could do anything you wanted, what would that be?"

"What was the hardest thing you did today?"

"Tell us something that makes you laugh."

"If you could be any animal, what would you be?"

"If you could visit any place, where would that be?"

"Tell us one thing that you like about the person on your left."

"What food do you love, and what food do you hate?"

"If you could have any three wishes, what would they be?"

"If you won a million dollars, what would you do?"

"What is the one chore that you hate the most?"

"If someone asked you to suggest a name for their new baby, what would it be?"

"What are some things you are thankful for?" Sometimes we take things for granted like our freedom, good hospitals and doctors, clean water, electricity, good friends, and family.

"Tell us a kind deed that you did today." Then compliment them for doing it. This small bit of recognition will help them feel happier. It will also reinforce their behavior and increase the chances of doing another kind deed sometime.

Consider doing this: Ask your family to add some questions to this list, print the list, cut out each question and put in a jar. At the beginning of dinner have someone draw a question. Then go around the table and have each person answer the question. Make family meals a regular occurrence.

Make Positive Deposits

In his book, *The 7 Habits of Highly Effective Families[1]*, Stephen R. Covey teaches how parents can improve relationships with their children by using the analogy of an Emotional Bank Account. By doing things that build trust in your relationship, you make deposits. By doing things that decrease the level of trust in your relationship, you make withdrawals. Examples of making withdrawals would be nagging, criticizing, and losing your temper.

If you have a high positive balance in this Emotional Bank Account, the level of trust is high, and communication is open and free and your ability to influence another person is increased dramatically. If you have a low balance or are overdrawn, there is little or no trust, no real communication, and no ability to work together to solve problems.

Children are watching you all the time, even if they appear not to be. They tend to follow your example. If you want your children to listen to you, listen to them. If you want your children to be kind, let them see you being kind. If you want your children to apologize after screwing up, then let them see you apologize after screwing up. If you are a good example, chances are, your children will be too. Here are some withdrawals and deposits you can make in your children's Emotional Bank Accounts.

Listening

Pretending to listen or listening while your mind is occupied with something else can be a withdrawal. Focusing all your attention on what someone is saying is a deposit. Really listening gives your child a sense that you feel he or she is important to you and a valued member of your family.

Being Kind

It's the little things that make a big difference. Saying cutting or sarcastic remarks is a withdrawal. On the other hand, words like *please, thank you, excuse me, may I help you, after you*, and *you look nice* are emotional deposits. Other deposits include doing small favors, calling just to say "hi", expressing appreciation, and giving sincere compliments. Tucking a note in a lunch box, writing a kind note on a mirror, fixing a favorite breakfast, and giving a hug or even a smile can be deposits.

Apologizing

Some parents think that apologizing shows weakness, when in fact, just the opposite is true. Apologizing turns withdrawals into deposits. "I said some things that were unkind and I want to apologize. I was angry and upset, but I should not have said what I did." We all make mistakes from time to time. When we do, we need to own up to it, sincerely apologize, and move on. The outcome will be far better than trying to hold on to stubborn pride.

Making and Keeping Promises

Making and breaking a promise is a huge withdrawal. Promises create excitement, anticipation and hope. Broken promises create disappointment and mistrust. It is better not to make a promise than to make one and break it. However, making and keeping promises are huge emotional deposits. If you make a promise to a child, do everything in your power to see it through.

Forgiving

Children give parents multiple opportunities every day to practice forgiveness, even if they never apologize. Forgiveness frees us from the burden that anger places on us. It releases bitterness and resentment we accumulate when other people (children in this case) are inconsiderate, uncooperative or rude. We can teach

51

children about apologizing, and we should, but we can choose to forgive (if only in our hearts) even when there is no hint of apology from the child. As children get older, they learn to apologize, and if they do, we as parents would do well to forgive, make that emotional deposit and move on.

Laughter

Besides strengthening your immune system, boosting your energy, and reducing stress, laughing together with your kids is a good bonding activity and an emotional deposit. Kids like being with people who make them feel good and laughing makes them (and you) feel good. Among the benefits of laughter that are shared between children and parents are these. Laughing with your children:

- strengthens relationships and promotes bonding
- allows kids to express their deeply felt emotions more freely
- gives kids a good dose of acceptance and a sense of belonging
- helps parents and children let go of anger and resentment
- makes parenting fun
- makes being a kid fun

If there was a pill that provided all the benefits of laughter, it would be in very high demand. Ask your kids if anything funny happened to them today. A good time to do this is at the dinner table, at family meetings, or after they've climbed into bed at night.

Of course it goes without saying that laughter must be shared by everyone. If someone is the brunt of a joke, then your laughter takes on the form of a major emotional withdrawal and harms your relationship – even if you say, "Just kidding."

Touching

Appropriate touching can be a powerful way to increase bonding, cooperation, and teamwork within our families. Babies actually need loving touch to develop properly, both physically and emotionally. As children grow, it can be hard to maintain a culture of touching, so here are some suggestions to get in the habit of touching.

- Give hugs. Make a routine out of hugging your children when they get up, when they're leaving for school, when they get home, before bed, or whenever it seems appropriate. A hug is a way to share both good and bad times. A hug can create a connection that words alone cannot.

- Children love to cuddle. Pile the whole family on the couch to watch TV instead of sitting in separate chairs. Cuddle together for bedtime stories.

- Use touch from time to time when listening, when celebrating an accomplishment, or rewarding good behavior. You can do a touch on the arm, a pat on the back, a fist bump, a high-five, or a hug.

- Offer your hand to help someone up off the floor.

- If you see someone coming up the stairs, offer you hand to help them up the last couple of steps.

Talking Together

Having a heart-felt, one-on-one conversation can be a huge deposit in someone's emotional bank account, and so satisfying for both parent and child. No hidden agenda, no advice, no criticism; just a little talking and a whole lot of listening.

Reading Together

Studies have shown that reading to your children helps them develop language skills, problem-solving skills, creativity and empathy. When they go to school, they tend to do better. Reading to children will bring the two of you closer together. You can start reading to children before they're even able to speak, and as they grow older, go to school and learn to read themselves, you can take turns reading. This is a good way for children to feel a positive sense of belonging, and a huge deposit in their emotional bank account. All you need is a library card, and it's free.

Saying I Love You

Some parents have a hard time saying, "I love you" to their children. Here are some things that happen to children when they hear "I love you". It makes them feel valuable. It gives them the freedom to make mistakes. It gives them confidence. It gives them courage. It helps them to love others. It makes them love you back more. You're missing an opportunity to make significant emotional deposits if you don't tell your children you love them.

Do Acts of Kindness with Your Children

Teach your children about doing acts of kindness, and then do them together. You will both receive four benefits:

1. You will cheer someone up, you will certainly surprise them, and you might change someone's life for the better.

2. You will both feel good – the kind of good you cannot feel any other way.

3. When you extend acts of kindness into to the universe, good things will find their way back to you.

4. By doing acts of kindness with someone else, you will strengthen your relationship with that person.

Anytime you do something to help someone or to cheer them up, you are doing an act of kindness. Here are a few suggestions of things you can do with your child.

Within Your Family
Do family member's chore.
Make a picture for someone.
Leave a kind note for someone.
Wash the car.
Make or buy a treat and share it.
Teach a skill you have become good at.

Help a younger sibling with homework.

Call or write to a grandparent.

Do the dishes even when it's not your turn.

Invite someone to play a board game with you.

Within Your Neighborhood

Mow someone's lawn.

Rake someone's leaves.

Shovel snow off someone's driveway or walks.

Bake cookies or a cake for someone.

Weed someone's flowerbed.

Walk the neighbor's dog.

For Anyone

Pay for a stranger's lunch or dinner at a restaurant.

Donate time to a local charity.

Return a shopping cart.

Send a handmade card to someone.

Send a care package to someone living away from home.

Offer your seat to someone.

Write a letter to someone thanking them for something they did.

Buy your friend some ice cream.

Help someone move in or out.

Assist someone who looks like they could use some help.

When everyone else is gossiping about someone, be the one who says something kind.

Let someone in the grocery store with only one or two items go ahead of you.

Put sticky notes with positive slogans on the mirrors in restrooms.

Hold the elevator for someone.

Help someone who is struggling with carrying something.

To get the most benefit from doing acts of kindness, expect nothing in return. One way to add to the fun is to do an act of kindness so nobody knows who did it. One exception to this is when you give someone food. People like to know where the food came from, so include a note or deliver it to them in person.

Use appropriate caution when it comes to doing acts of kindness for people you don't know. Do not let your child approach strangers alone.

Chapter 7 - Principle #4 - Acknowledge Negative Feelings

If you were to ask me, "what is one thing that I can do that will have a significant positive impact on my children's behavior?", here is what I would tell you: "When children come to you with hurt feelings, instead of denying or discounting their feelings, instead of criticizing or offering advice, give your children the freedom to say all kinds of nasty, critical things, whether they are true or not. Then let them know you understand how they feel."

During all my reading and research on child behavior, I learned many different opinions on how to get children to behave. One thing that child behavior experts seem to agree on is that children need to be heard, and they need to feel understood, and it is not until children do feel heard and understood, that they are likely to change.

It isn't until children's feelings are heard and acknowledged, that they are free to change.

Some parents believe that if they allow their kids to express their anger and negative feelings, their kids will act out those feelings and their behavior will get worse. Actually the opposite is true. Parents who allow their children to express their anger and negative feelings will be helping them to "let go" of those feelings. As a result, they will feel better and behave better.

When a child comes to you with a problem, hurt feelings, or something that is bothering him, and you can tell he's feeling angry, frustrated, discouraged, sad, or a host of other negative emotions, how do you respond to that child? It could make a big difference in your relationship. The discussion could end in an argument or a misunderstanding that leaves the child more upset and discouraged than when the discussion began. Or, the discussion could end with the child feeling much better and your relationship being made stronger, in which case the child will feel more comfortable opening up to you in the future.

When children come to you in distress, they are not coming to hear your opinion, your point of view, or your advice. They are coming to you to feel understood. If you listen, really listen, it gives them a sense that you understand, and that will cause them to feel less upset, less confused, be able to cope with their problems, and even come up with solutions on their own.

When you give your children a chance to talk about what's bothering them, and acknowledge their feelings (sometimes called empathy, or an "empathetic" response), they feel cared about and comforted. They feel free to open up and tell you more. That might not seem so hard, but if you listen to the typical talk between parents and children you'll notice that it's common practice for parents to **deny** their children's feelings. "You don't really mean that." "That's a terrible thing to say." Most of us grew up having our feelings denied. When we tried to express our hurt feelings, we were criticized and told how to think. So it's natural for us, as parents, to do the same thing with our children.

The way we respond to our children's feelings makes a difference in how they feel, and that makes a difference in how they behave. When kids feel understood they behave better. However, it is natural for parents to listen with the intent to respond rather than listen with the intent to understand. They are either talking or thinking about what to say. For example:

Child: "I never want to see Emily again."
Parent: "Nonsense. You don't really mean that."
Child: "My teacher sucks."
Parent: "That's not a very nice thing to say."
Child: "I'm bored."
Parent: "Are you kidding – with all those toys?"

When we deny our children's feelings it makes them feel frustrated and angry. But when we give our children an empathetic response, it makes them feel accepted, understood, and leads to problem solving.

Let's say your child comes to you and says, "My teacher chewed me out and embarrassed me in front of the whole class. I hate her." What would be your response? Parents who do not know how to give an empathetic response might respond in one of the following ways:

Denying Feelings: "You're making a big deal out of nothing. The other kids probably didn't even care, and tomorrow no one will even remember."

Giving Advice: "Sounds like you better stay off her radar by following directions. Then you won't have to go through that again."

The Philosophical Response: "Sometimes life is like that. People are going to dump on you and you've got to learn to get over it."

Taking the Other Person's Side: "Well, she's a young teacher. She probably didn't even know she embarrassed you. And if she did know, she probably had a good reason for it."

Asking Questions: "What exactly did you do that caused her to do that? Did you fail to do your homework? Was it your behavior? Does she embarrass other kids too, or just you?"

Psychoanalysis: "Do you think maybe you're mad because you messed up and got caught? Perhaps what you're feeling is guilt."

Offering Pity: "Oh my gosh. That's terrible. Come here, give me a hug."

I'll fix it: "The nerve of that lady, thinking she can embarrass my son like that. I'm going to march down there tomorrow and let her know in no uncertain terms she is never to do that again. Better yet, I'll go straight to the principal and insist she gets reprimanded."

Here's an Empathetic Response: (An attempt to tune into another person's feelings) "In front of the whole class? That must have been very embarrassing."

The empathetic response should do nothing else but show that you understand what the other person is *feeling*. It is not agreeing, disagreeing, offering a solution, or giving your opinion. And it is certainly not telling the other person he shouldn't feel the way he does.

In their book, *How To Talk So Kids Will Listen & How to Listen so Kids Will Talk*[1], authors Adele Faber and Elaine Mazlish make what they call a tremendous discovery: "The more you try to push a child's unhappy feelings away, the more he becomes stuck with them. The more comfortably you can accept the bad feelings, the easier it is for kids to let go of them. I guess you could say that if you want to have a happy family, you'd better be prepared to permit the expression of a lot of unhappiness."

Only after a child believes that the parent understands what he is feeling, does the child feel less upset, and more able to find a solution to his problem – even if the solution is to do nothing.

Sometimes simply listening to a child with your full attention is all it takes for the child to feel better. Full attention means we focus on listening, not on what we are going to say next. We should listen with the intent to understand, not with the intent to respond. Consider using these three steps to help children feel understood:

1. Give your full attention to listening.

2. Show that you are listening with "Oh", "Mmm", "I see" or nodding.

3. Identify the emotion and put it into a sentence.

Depending on the situation, you may not even get to Step 3, because after using the first two steps, your child may feel good enough to conclude your conversation.

Here are two examples of the way parents can respond to a child in distress. Each example shows the **common way** and the **empathetic way**. In these two examples the empathetic way will focus only on the first two steps: 1) Give your full attention to listening, and 2) Show that you are listening with "Oh", "Mmm", "I see" or nodding.

Common way:

Child: "Sage pushed me."

Parent: "Why can't you kids just get along? You go tell Sage that if there's any more trouble, I'm sending everybody home."

Empathetic way:

Child: "Sage pushed me."

Parent: "Oh?"

Child: "We were running to get the ball and she pushed me so I wouldn't get it."

Parent: "Mmmm."

Child: "And I fell down and got hurt."

Parent: "I see."

Child: "I'm not going play with Sage any more. I'm going to play with Anna.

Sometimes it can be just that easy. Children just need to vent their feelings, and after they do, they solve the problem themselves and leave feeling better.

Common way:

Child: "Someone stole my eraser."

Parent: "Are you sure you didn't lose it? Did you check your backpack?"

Child: "I got up to get a drink and when I got back it was gone."

Parent: "That's the third time you've lost an eraser this year. You have to learn to take care of your things. I will buy you one more but this is the last time. If you lose this one, you're out of luck.

Empathetic way:

Child: "Someone stole my eraser."

Parent: "Oh?"

Child: "I got up to get a drink and when I got back it was gone."

Parent: "Mmm."

Child: "This is the third time I lost my eraser."

Parent: (nodding).

Child: "From now on when I get up to go somewhere, I 'm going to take my eraser with me.

When parents listen with full attention and show they are listening with "Oh", "Mmm", "I see" and nodding, children feel safe to express their feelings without fear of a lecture or a scolding. They also feel inclined to explore solutions to their problem. Now let's examine *Step 3, Identify the emotion and put it into a sentence*. Here are some possible emotions (or feelings):

Shocking – "That must have been a shock."

Tough – "That's got to be tough." (This is a good generic response when you have to think fast.)

Frustrating – "That must have been so frustrating."

Discouraging – "How discouraging."

Devastated – "Really? You must be devastated."

Angry – "You sound angry."

Mad – "You're THAT mad at him."

Annoying – "It's annoying to have to put up with that."

Furious – "Boy, you must be furious after what she did."

Disappointing – "That must have been disappointing."

Upset – "I see something is making you upset."

Hurt – "Losing a friend can really hurt."

Scary – "The first day of school can be scary."

Unhappy – "You seem unhappy about it."

Embarrassing – "Being laughed at can be so embarrassing."

Hoping – "You were hoping to get it over with."

Don't like – "Wow. You really don't like your new teacher."

Doubt – "You're having doubts about going."

Sad – "Having a pet die is so sad."

Okay, here's the skill. While your distressed child is describing his troubles, you need to watch his gestures, listen to his words, and decide which of the above emotions he is feeling. Then use it in a sentence. Here are some examples:

Common way:

Child: "Carter is moving away"

Dad: "Don't worry, you have lots of friends, and you can email each other."

Child: "But it's not the same. We can't hang out together".

Dad: "Well, life is tough, son. Sometimes bad things happen."

Child: "You don't get it, dad. I'll never have a friend like that again."

Dad: "You might think so now, but down the road you'll make new friends to hang out with and probably even forget about Carter."

Child: "Never mind, I'm outa here."

Empathetic way:

Child: "Carter is moving away."

Dad: "Oh no. <u>What a shock</u>."

Child: "We'll never be able to hang out together."

Dad: "You two were best friends. <u>That's got to be tough</u>."

Child: "I'll never have another friend like him, ever."

Dad: "Mmm."

Child: "It's like we can read each other's mind. We know what the other is going to say."

Dad: "And now he's moving. <u>That's sad</u>."

Child: "I guess there's always email, skype, and I could go visit him, right? I got to go call Carter. Thanks, dad."

Some parents fear that verbalizing a feeling will make it worse. Just the opposite is true. When a child hears the words that identify what he is feeling, he feels comforted. Don't worry about choosing the wrong emotion. If you do, your child will correct you:

"You must feel angry."

"Not so much angry as I am disappointed that I can't trust her anymore."

"I see."

Common way:

Child: "I'm not cleaning my room."

Mom: "And why not?"

Child: "Because."

Mom: "Well, I'm sorry, but you should have thought about that when you made the mess."

Child: (Starts crying)

Mom: "Now go up there and get started."

Child: (Sits on the floor, folds her arms and cries louder)

Mom: (Grabs her arm, and takes her to her room) "Now don't come out until this room is clean. Do you understand?"

Child: (Continues crying) "But why, mom?"

Mom: "Because I said so."

Empathetic way:

Child: "I'm not cleaning my room."

Mom: "Oh?"

Child: (Is silent)

Mom:(Is silent but turns her whole attention to the child. Nods as if to say, "You have my attention, go on.")

Child: "I'm not cleaning my room."

Mom: "Sounds to me like you're upset."

Child: "I'm not cleaning my room."

Mom: "I see. You really sound mad."

Child: (Starts to cry) "There's too much."

Mom: "Oooh. There's such a big mess that you're discouraged, like it might take you forever."

Child: "It will."

Mom: "Hmm."

Child:(Crying)

Mom: (Is silent)

Child: "Can you help me?"

Mom: "I'll tell you what. I'll help you clean for one minute. We will both clean as fast as we can. I mean super-hero fast. Then I have to finish dinner."

Child: "Okay, mom." (Takes mom's hand and pulls her toward the bedroom)

Hold off on giving advice or solving the problem. This mom could easily have said, "Would you like me to help you?" But that would have taken away the learning opportunity for the child to solve the problem herself. If the child never got around to asking for help, then obviously, it would have been reasonable for mom to ask if she could help. Do you think that when mom used the empathetic way of responding, the child felt more respected, more accepted, and more understood than with the common way of responding? Does is make sense that when feelings are denied, there is more tension and hostility between child and parent?

In the example above, after the child has finished cleaning her room to mom's satisfaction, mom can take advantage of a teaching opportunity:

Mom: "How do you feel now that your room is done?"

Child: "Good."

Mom: "How did you feel before you started cleaning?"

Child: "Bad."

Mom: "Will I always be able to help you clean your room?"

Child: "Probably not."

Mom: "So what can you do so you don't feel so bad about cleaning your room?"

Child: "I don't know."

Mom: "Think hard."

Child: "Maybe not let it get so messy?"

Mom: "Good answer. I think you've got it. High five." (Mom and daughter high five each other)

By now you've probably guessed that dealing with feelings is more of an art than a science. This new "responding skill" can feel awkward at first. You will go through some trial and error. The important thing is that you keep trying. Because if you give up and revert back to your old habits (the common way of responding), your children will seek understanding from someone else. And that someone else may not be the kind of person you want your kids to hang around with. Here's one more example:

Dad: "Hi son. How was your day?"

Son: "It sucked! And I don't want to talk about it."

Dad: "Sounds like it must have been disappointing."

Son: "It was worse than that. It was terrible."

Dad: "Why? What happened?"

Son: "The coach posted a list of everyone who was on the team. I wasn't on it. I was cut from the team. I thought I'd be first string. I didn't even make second string and I'm better than most of the guys that tried out."

Dad: "You were cut from the team? Oh my gosh, what a shock."

Son: "That's not the worst of it. Mike and Joe made the cut. They're on the team and I'm not. They're going to be at practice while I'm going to be… I don't know. I hate it!"

Dad: "Hmmm."

Dad will keep listening until his son has had time to vent. He'll refrain from giving advice unless his son asks for it. He will show that he is listening with "Oh", "Mmm", "I see" and nodding.

What if you notice your child is sad or upset about something? How would you initiate the conversation? I'm going to suggest against saying, "What's eating you?" Instead, I'm going to recommend something better. Describe what you see. "I see something is making you sad." Or, "you really seem upset."

I think you'll discover, as I did, that you will have many opportunities to acknowledge negative feelings, and that this skill will become one of your favorites.

Chapter 8 - Principle #5 - Teach Life Skills

As a parent, what is it that you want to ultimately accomplish? My guess is that you want to see to it that your child learns to become an independent adult, with the knowledge and ability to take good care of him or herself when the time comes to leave the nest. And as your child progresses, you will take pleasure in watching and participating in each accomplishment along the way. Shouldn't that be the goal of every parent?

As important as that goal seems to be, it is my observation that many young adults are incapable of taking care of themselves because they have not been trained. Instead, their parents do everything for them and deny them learning opportunities that would help them become independent, happy adults.

I see two reasons for this. 1) Parents feel that the way to communicate love for their children is by doing everything for their children that they should be capable of doing on their own. 2) Parents get worn down by the whining and complaining, and feel it is just easier to do for their children rather than make them do it themselves. In both cases, the parents are focusing on the moment, and not on the big picture.

In her book, *The Parenting Breakthrough*[1], Merrilee Brown Boyack talks about over nurturing children. She says, "parents who nurture too much convey messages like these to their children: "You can't do this because –

you're not smart enough.

you're not reliable enough.

you're not old enough.

you're not responsible enough.

you're *just* a child.

I don't trust you.

I don't believe in you.

you're not capable of taking care of yourself.

the quality of your work is inadequate.

only women do these kinds of things.

only men do these kinds of things.

moms do all the dirty work." (conveying a serious lack of respect for women)

Contrast this with parents who keep their children's future in mind. They love their children and want them to be happy, but rather than doing everything for them, they train their children in age-related skills and watch their children learn, struggle, make mistakes, figure it out and eventually master those skills. They watch their children's self-esteem go up as they take on the belief that "I can do this myself". They watch their children's self-confidence grow as they take steps to becoming capable and independent.

As parents teach their kids life skills, they won't have to worry about making them happy because their kids will learn to make themselves happy. And isn't that what we ultimately want for them?

Children lack vision. That's why they have parents. Many children think that sitting around watching TV or playing video games all day is the best way to be happy. Our role as parents is to take charge and be a leader. Our role is to train our children to be independent adults someday and give us grandchildren. Then we can spoil all we want because that's what grandparents do. But until then, we need to give our children the principles, knowledge and ability to succeed in a tough world.

As a take-charge parent (or the boss of your kids), you are going to experience frustration as your children resist and ask, "But why do I have to?" You will look them in the eye and say, "Because I have more information and experience than you do, and I know what you're going to be up against when you strike out on your own. So, you can take comfort in knowing that I will do everything I can to get you prepared." They'll say, "But why?" and that's when you'll say, "Because I said so." Your children don't know it, but you are going to give them a gift that will benefit them for the rest of their lives, the gift of knowledge and ability; the gift of independence.

Life skills are skills that help children make the transition from dependence to independence by adding to their capabilities. From putting toys in the toy box to mowing the lawn, life skills prepare a child to be productive. When you teach children life skills you empower them. You give them the ability, the confidence, and the "power" to do something they couldn't do before. There are many benefits to empowering your children. They would include:

- It instills in them a sense of accomplishment and confidence.

- It enables them to be a more capable, contributing member of the family, thus satisfying their need to feel a sense of belonging.

- It increases their sense of personal power so they don't feel they have to be sassy or defiant to meet that need on their own.

- It helps them to become more independent.

- It prepares them to be a productive member of society.

- It gives them skills they will need as adults.

- It could begin an interest in something that turns into a passion.

- They learn at a younger age with your help than they would without your help.

- It bonds them, or brings them closer to the person who taught them.

- The more they learn to do, the less mom and dad have to do for them.

- It increases good behavior and decreases bad behavior.

Life skills include household responsibilities, but go beyond that. They include anything that enriches someone's life such as learning to count, throwing a ball, riding a bike, making a healthy smoothie, learning to swim, or riding a horse. As children are exposed to life skills, they will decide what interests them and what doesn't. Keep in mind that what interests you may not necessarily interest them. And what interests one child might not interest another. Exposing them to many life skills will give them opportunities to *choose* what they like and what they don't like, and being able to *choose* helps satisfy their need for a sense of personal power.

Children are hard-wired with a need for a sense of belonging and personal power. Teaching them life skills is a good way to satisfy both needs in positive ways. We give them a sense of belonging by spending time teaching them. We give them personal power by empowering them with new skills.

I believe every child is born with unique, talents and gifts, and the more we expose our children to new life skills, the greater the chance that those unique gifts will be discovered. For example, a child may be born with the gift of singing. But unless that child is exposed to opportunities to sing, that gift may never be realized.

Sometimes parents don't attempt to train their children to do something because it's faster, less frustrating, and done better if they just do it themselves. But then both the children and the parents lose out on the benefits of empowerment.

Four-year-old Tyler tried pouring milk from a gallon plastic jug and poured more on the table than in his cup. He looked at Dad, fearful of being yelled at. "That's okay," said Dad. "Let's clean it up together."

Dad got a sponge and started to mop up the milk. "Here, use this," he said to Tyler. Tyler finished sponging up the mess.

"I have an idea," said Dad. "Let's play the pouring game. He found a pitcher and poured the remaining milk from the jug into the pitcher and put the pitcher in the refrigerator. Then he rinsed out the jug and put an inch of water in it. He took the jug and a cup over to the table.

"I want you to pour this water into this cup," Dad said to Tyler. The jug was light and Tyler had little trouble as he slowly poured. "Hey, you did it!" said Dad. "Now let's put a little more water in the jug and try it again." He filled the jug up half way with water.

"Don't worry about spilling," he said. "After all, this is the pouring game and it's okay to spill. Let's see how you do. Tyler picked up the jug, tipped it and spilled all over the table. "That was a good try," said Dad. "Try again."

Tyler practiced. Dad emptied his cup and Tyler practiced some more. Dad told him how good he was getting. Then filled the jug to the top and gave it to Tyler. It was heavy now. He learned to tip the jug without picking it up. Each time he practiced, he learned a little more about pouring.

The pouring game was also a good way for Dad to teach Tyler that it was okay to try and fail. When you fail, you learn. Each time Tyler got a little better at pouring, he felt more confident. He couldn't wait to show his mother.

As Tyler learns new things, his confidence grows. As his confidence grows, he becomes less afraid and more eager to learn more new things. Would Tyler have eventually learned to pour from a jug by himself? Sure. But by teaching him this life skill, mom and dad get all the empowering benefits described at the beginning of this chapter sooner than later.

The Training Plan

The remainder of this chapter is going to help you create a "training plan" that you will use to train your kids to be capable and empowered. A training plan like this may be new to you. It is to many parents. You will begin putting this training plan together (with your spouse if applicable) by making a list of the life-skills you think your children need to learn. It will be a work in progress. You will constantly modify, adjust, and add new life-skills to your list.

Imagine sending your child into to world knowing how to do such things as shop for food, cook, write checks, pay bills, change a flat tire, do laundry, iron clothes, wash dishes, clean the oven, budget money, understand debit and credit cards, make repairs, vote, sell items on the internet, mend clothing, properly treat a spouse, raise a family, and make a living. All these adult skills start with learning important life-skills at a young age – such skills as dressing oneself, picking up toys, setting the table, making one's own lunch, emptying the dishwasher, baking cookies, and filling the car with gas. You will not have to worry about your child leaving home with crucial gaps in experience and knowledge that would prevent him or her from having a successful adult life. Your children will be forever grateful for your efforts, and your legacy will continue through generations.

Start by making a list of every skill you can think of that your children need to be able to do to become independent adults. Don't worry about making it complete. You will add to it and modify it over time. Assign each skill to an age group at which time your child will be old enough to understand and do it. Keep in mind that each child is different. One could be ahead or behind the way you organize your age groups. Some kids learn faster than others. Some are more motivated than others. So we are going to keep our plan flexible and simple. If you have children who are old enough to learn skills that they should have learned already, then you have some catching up to do.

Following is a list of life skills to get you started, but don't assume it covers everything. The list is organized by age group. After you have made your own list, we will go over what to do with it.

Ages 2-3

Put away toys
Get dressed
Use the toilet without help
Put dirty clothes in the hamper
Take plates to kitchen sink after eating
Set the table with help
Begin to brush teeth
Carry in the mail
Wash and dry hands – will require a stool
Put clean silverware away
Count to 10
Kick a soft, inflatable ball
Say please and thank you
Stay away from the street
Cross the street safely with an adult

Ages 4-5

Tie shoes
Recite full name, address and phone number
What to do if a stranger approaches you
What to do if there is a fire
Use the phone
Make a 911 call

Clear the dinner table and wipe it down after a meal
Put toys away when done playing with them
Feed the family pet
Set the table independently
Fold towels
Brush teeth and comb hair without assistance
Water plants
Help vacuum
Use good table manners
Ride a bike – wear a bike helmet, cross the street safely
Count to 100
Read
Tell time
Make a paper airplane
Draw a picture

Ages 6-7

Make a sandwich
Use the stove – heat up a can of food
Rinse, dry, and put dishes away
Empty the dishwasher
Make the bed
Vacuum without help
Use an alarm to get up in the morning
Bathe him/herself, dry off with a towel, hang the towel up
Take a shower
Pump up a bicycle tire
Properly greet an adult
Shake hands (with a firm grip)
Count money
Change a light bulb

Run the microwave

Wrap a present

Do homework without constant supervision

Play a musical instrument

Play simple board games

Throw a ball and catch with a mitt – underhanded at
close range

Whistling

Arithmetic

Origami

Tie a knot

Begin piano lessons

Make the traffic lights turn green by snapping their
fingers

Skip flat stones on a lake

Ages 8-9

Wash the dishes or fill the dishwasher

Fold clothes and put them away

Use a broom and dustpan

Clean a toilet

Mop the floor

Take the trash out

Make a simple meal like macaroni and cheese

Bake cookies

Take a written phone message

Plant, water and weed a garden

Fish

Fill a car with gas

Wash and vacuum a car

Order for yourself at a restaurant

Knit a scarf

Perform a simple magic trick

Have a savings account

Use email

Write and send letters

Learn the dangers of alcohol, drugs and tobacco and what to do when offered

Ages 10-13

Use the internet (with a filter)

Use a sewing machine

Change bed sheets

Plunge a toilet

Clean the oven

Make bread

Understand basic nutrition

Understand weight control

Use the washing machine and dryer

Use a newspaper and flyers to find bargains and coupons

Shop for food

Prepare meals and desserts from a recipe book

Learn meat handling rules and food handling basics

Iron clothes

Tie a necktie

Hammer nails

Use power tools

Mow the lawn

Use a weed whacker

Paint a wall

Take the Red Cross babysitting course

Learn first aid – certify for CPR

Babysit with an adult nearby

Build a camp fire

Use a pay phone

Place a long distance call

Place a collect call

Be able to apply practical math skills

Wardrobe matching

Make and keep dentist appointments

Juggling

Yo-yo-ing

Hula hooping

Type without looking

Budget money

Pay household bills

Understand debit and credit cards, interest and debt

Order something on the internet

Sell something on the internet

Understand prescriptions

Start to learn computer programs like the Microsoft Office Suite

Ages 14-16

Learn basic household repairs

Memorize Social Security Number

Accompany parent to vote

Accompany parent to register a car

Learn how car insurance works

Change a flat tire

Jump a car with a dead battery

Check tire pressure and oil in a car, and top off windshield fluid

Understand a car's maintenance schedule

Understand what a car's warning lights mean

Perform thorough car detailing

Learn the rules of the road

Learn to drive

Learn about hair, makeup, jewelry, fingernail painting (girls)

Create a resume, cover letter, and learn how to interview

Open a checking account

Incredible, isn't it? Not until we sit down and make a list, do we realize how much someone needs to know to be a successful, independent adult; and there's so much more that can be added to the list depending on your family. Your list might even inspire *you* to learn something new. Hey, it's never too late! Go over this list with your spouse to see what else needs to be included. Then make a copy for each child. Our next step is to unveil the Training Plan to your children.

Unveiling the Training Plan

Okay, you've got this massive list and you're feeling totally overwhelmed. You were just coming to terms with spending daily personal time with each of your children, and now this. Don't worry. You will be amazed at how well this fits into your family schedule and the benefits you will receive by having your children trained in these life skills.

Unveil your new Training Plan in a family meeting. Gather everyone together and say, "Kids, we have been thinking about your future. We know what you are going to be up against when you strike out on your own someday and we want you to be prepared. So we have made a list of some skills we feel you'll need to have." Some kids will grumble, some will show interest, some will be too young to understand. Give a copy of your list to each child and go over the list with them. You'll get all sorts of reactions.

Remind them *why* they need to learn these skills: to become happy, successful independent adults, capable of taking care of themselves and their own family. When kids learn the "why" of things, they are more apt to buy in to the idea. Okay, maybe not all the time but sometimes it works.

It will be interesting to go through their lists and cross off everything they already know how to do, and add new skills they would like to learn. Identify the skills they should be learning now, and the ones they should be learning over the next six months. Some children will be excited to get started right away. Others, not so much. Don't get into an argument. It's enough at this point just to introduce the Training Plan.

Putting the Training Plan into Action

Choose who you want to do the training. Yes, parents will do most of the training but that doesn't always have to be the case. It can be mom, dad, an older sibling, an aunt, uncle, neighbor, Boy Scout or Girl Scout troop. Whoever it is, you are still responsible for the training to be done right, so you need to be sure the child is learning what you expect.

Who do you know who could teach your child how to take care of a bicycle? Do you have a neighbor who is a soccer player who can teach your child the ins and outs of kicking and passing? Can grandma teach how to plant a garden? Can grandpa teach how to fish? Can you go to a teacher or a scout leader and ask that they teach a lesson on table manners? Can Aunt Christine teach how to change a tire? Yes, there is nothing more effective in crushing a stereotype than a girl teaching "guy stuff" and a guy teaching "girl stuff". Can dad teach how to make chocolate chip cookies? Do you have a friend or neighbor who loves to sew? Don't feel you are imposing. People are usually flattered that you'd think so highly of them as to ask them to teach your child something they are good at.

Do you have a child who could teach their younger bother the finer points of cleaning the toilet? Boys who learn to clean the toilet are inclined to aim more accurately knowing they will have to clean later. You can tap into a wide variety of people from your family, neighborhood, school, church, social clubs, and so on.

Ensure your child's safety. Make sure the person you ask to train your child is someone you know and trust, and that your child will never be totally alone with that person.

Then both you and your children will take delight in your children showing you what they learned. Not only will your kids learn something new from another person, but they will feel good that another person felt they were important enough to take time to train them. Don't forget to have the child write a thank-you letter.

Depending on the skill being taught, more than one training session may be required until the child understands thoroughly. While training, be very specific. Demonstrate just how clean a dish should be before going into the dishwasher. When showing how to clean windows and mirrors, explain how to get into the corners. When showing how to sweep the kitchen floor, explain how moving the chairs away from the kitchen table makes it easier to sweep under the table. When training how to clean a bedroom, explain exactly what you expect: All toys go in the toy box. Pick up everything off the floor and put it where it belongs. Make your bed. Close all your dresser drawers. Nothing goes on the closet floor except shoes and the laundry basket. Clean out from under your bed.

Remember that this is training and kids will make mistakes. *Do not criticize imperfection.* Be patient. You may be a pro at a particular life skill, but your child is new at it and will want to withdraw if she feels that you are impatient. Instead of saying, "that's not how I taught you to make your bed," say, "good effort on the bed. I notice you got the wrinkles out, but what could you do to make this bedspread a little straighter?" Point out what they did well (I notice you got the wrinkles out) and then *ask* what they could do make a specific improvement (but what could you do to make this bedspread a little straighter?)

When you ask instead of tell, it helps your child develop problem-solving skills. If the child doesn't know the answer to the question, you can say, "Let me make a suggestion…" If the child really messes up, say, "That's okay. You're just learning. It's okay to mess up. Keep trying. You'll get it with a little more practice."

Now if a child has been practicing a skill for a while and starts to get lazy or doesn't meet expectations, refrain from criticizing: "Son, that's not how I trained you to wash clothes. What's the matter with you?" Instead, go back to teaching mode and say, "Son, remember when I taught you about doing laundry?

What did I say about separating colors?" "And why do you suppose I told you that?" Don't criticize. Ask questions. Teach.

Earlier we talked about rewarding good behavior. Treat learning a new skill the same way and give a verbal reward: "It looks nice. Good job." But don't overdo it: "Wow, what a great job. You really picked that up fast. Hey everyone! Come see what a fabulous job Elisabeth did dusting the dresser." Resist the urge to exaggerate her accomplishment. She will come to appreciate your good judgment more if you do not go bonkers over her achievement.

Some training only takes a couple of minutes. Teach a child to call 911: Have the child dial the number while the phone is hung up. Then call a friend who is expecting your call. "911. What is your emergency? What is your name? What is your address?" Boom! Done.

Teach a child how to handle a stranger at the door when mom and dad are gone: Knock knock. Shhh. Don't make a sound. Don't open the door. Done. Teach a child to feed the dog: Scoop out the food with a cup. Fill the water bowl half way. Done – and you are on your way to empowering your children and reaping the benefits.

Once children learn a new skill, have them take responsibility for it. Let them make the skill a part of their lives. Don't do it for them. Once they've learned to dress themselves, tie their shoes, feed the pet, do dishes, clean their bedroom, pick out their clothes, wash their clothes, iron their clothes, or fix snacks, let them. Many of their new skills will turn into daily or weekly chores. Then, if you occasionally decide to do something for the child that he has mastered, you'll be doing it out of kindness, love and caring.

Teaching children life skills might seem like a lot of work, but in the long run, the rewards will be worth it. No longer will your children run to you with an urgent request, "Mom, can you hurry and wash this?" or "Can you iron this for me?" or "I'm hungry. Can you make me a snack?" Your children will know how to take care of their clothes, handle money, cook, and keep rooms clean. Their self-esteem will be a reflection of their self-sufficiency. They will learn how consequences are a result of their actions or in-actions. And when the time comes, they will be better prepared for the work force and to have a family of their own.

Children love to help at a young age. Take advantage of that. Have him help you with a recipe by cracking an egg into a bowl. Have him help you take out the garbage by holding on to the garbage bag while you both take it out to the trash can. Have him help sweep the floor by holding the dust pan. When a child says, "can I try that?" Consider making that a teaching moment.

Assign Chores

Most kids hate chores. If you feel like a bad parent because you have a hard time getting kids to do chores, take comfort in knowing that kids everywhere consider chores to be a major disruption of their recreation time. But every day, kids need to do something to contribute to the family. Chores are family contributions that always happen to be inconvenient. Some parents even prefer to call chores "family contributions."

As a parent, you know that "work" is a necessary part of a child's healthy development, and household work (or chores) trains a child to be responsible, not to mention lightening everyone else's load around the home. When a child grows up and goes off to make a living in a challenging world, the work he learned at home will serve as a foundation to how he performs on the job and in his own home. So, how in the world do you get kids to do chores with a minimum amount of drama?

First, you, as a parent, must be firm. Do not give in to your children's methods of dodging opportunities to do chores no matter how incredibly creative or persuasive they are. Some parents give up trying to convince their children to do chores because it is easier to just do it themselves. Sometimes children will complain longer than it would take to actually do the task. This can be challenging for parents. But once your kids come to understand that your determination is stronger than theirs, they will stop resisting so much.

One day my daughter went off to school without having done her chore assignment, which was to wash dishes. My wife drove to school, checked my daughter out, and brought her home to finish her chore. To this day, she still remembers that. It was as hard on my wife as it was on my daughter. I am happy to report that my daughter is now an excellent mother and homemaker. If you place serious value on chores, your children will come to value them too. Oh, and if you are wondering, after that incident, my daughter was pretty good at finishing what chores she needed to do before school. The other children were better too.

Second, your children should be thoroughly trained to do the chores they are assigned. That is, they should be able to do them and know exactly what is expected, and they should be expected to do a good job.

Third, make a list of all the chores that need to be done. A good time to do this is during a family meeting where you can get everyone's input. I remember when we did this. I gathered the family together and said, "Tonight we are going to make a list of everything that needs to be done to keep our family running smoothly." That produced some eye-rolling and moaning among the children. I continued, "I need your help in identifying everything that needs to be done." We started our list. Most of the suggestions came from me and my wife, but we were open to any input, whether it was positive or negative.

Then we made assignments. It was agreed that dad would make the money, and mom would do the shopping and cook the meals. We divided up the rest of the tasks among all of us. Doing dishes was unanimously the worst chore. We assigned 2 people on that task. We decided how often the chores would change and came up with a chart. We started on a daily chart that turned into a weekly chart. We bundled chores differently from time to time. The point is, we adjusted the chores according to how we felt would work best at the time, a what the children wanted to try.

Here is what some parents do to get their kids to do chores. Some parents decide to let their kids divide the chores among themselves. That way the kids take on the chores they would rather do, and get creative splitting up the chores they don't like. Some parents decide to give a deadline for the chores to be completed and then if the deadline is not met, the parents do the work. Then later, when the child wants one of them to do something, the parent will say, "I'm sorry. I did your chore and now I have no time or energy left."

Offer Choices

Making decisions gives kids a sense of personal power. When parents offer their kids a choice, it gives them an opportunity to make a decision. So a good way to help kids feel a sense of positive personal power is to offer choices.

Give your kids a choice whenever you would normally choose something for them. Instead of giving them a breakfast cereal, off them a choice: "Would you like this cereal or this cereal?" Or ask for their opinion: "Which soap should I put by the sink, the bar soap or the squirt soap?" Offer two choices, each of which you like. Here are some more examples:

Do you want potato chips or corn chips in your lunch?

Do you want the green towel or the blue towel?

Do you want juice or milk?

Which outfit do you want to wear, this one or this one?

Shall we read this book or this book?

Do you want to brush your teeth first or shall I brush your teeth first?

Do you want to go to the park before or after lunch?

Shall we have sloppy-joes or grilled cheese sandwiches?

Shall we go to the post office or the bank first?

Offering choices is a simple but powerful way to give kids daily doses of personal power. You can also use choices to get kids to do something they don't want to do:

Do you want to load the dishwasher or clean up dog poop?

Would you like to clean the living room or the bathroom?

Do you want to do your homework at the table or up to the counter?

Do you want to take a bath or a shower?

Do you want to brush your teeth in the bathroom or the kitchen?

Would you like to go home now or in 10 minutes?

If your child cannot make up her mind, you can say, "If you don't choose, then I will choose for you." If your child chooses something that was not one of the choices, you can make the choice for her.

Parent: "Do you want milk or water?"
Child: "soda pop".
Parent: "Water it is."

Make Your House Kid-Friendly

There are physical changes you can make around the house to help your kids become more responsible, more independent, and feel a sense of empowerment. As your kids learn to take on more responsibility, you will feel less need to micromanage. When trying to get your kids to change a behavior, ask yourself if there are any changes you could make around the house that would help. Here are some suggestions to get you started.

- Post a list of everything that needs to be done when cleaning the bedroom: put dirty clothes in hamper, clean out from under bed, closet floor should be clean except for shoes, vacuum carpet, etc. The children will be responsible for completing everything on the list and require less reminding from you.

- Post a list of everything that a child might need to take to school depending on the day. The list would include lunchbox, homework, permission slip, gym clothes, mittens, etc. It would be the child's responsibility to look over the list every morning before leaving for school to make sure nothing is forgotten.

- Designate a shelf, cubby or box for everything that needs to be taken to school. Everything the child needs to take to school can be put there the night before to eliminate the stress of trying to find everything when being rushed out the door.

- Give your child a wristwatch. Then when she is at a friend's house and needs to be home by a certain time, she can easily watch the time.

- Put cereal, after-school snacks, and other things that kids need regularly in a place low enough where they can have access to it without your help.

- Provide a lower rod in a closet where kids can get and hang up their clothes without help.

- Provide smaller containers for milk, juice and water to allow kids to pour without spilling.

Teach Problem-Solving

Parents often take it upon themselves to solve their children's problems, which results in a missed opportunity to teach the skill of problem-solving. I attended a Love And Logic® workshop where one of the sessions was about training children to solve their own problems. It got me thinking about how important it is that children learn to solve problems when their problems are small so that when they grow up and have big problems, they are prepared to deal with them.

Here's how it works. Let's say your child comes to you with a problem: "I can't find my coat." "I have no clean clothes!" "I suck at basketball." "I'm failing math". Here are five simple steps to help you guide your children through the problem-solving process.

Step 1. Show empathy.

Empathy is explained in Chapter 7, Principle #4 – Acknowledge Negative Feelings. "Oh no, that's got to make you mad." "Oh man, I'll bet that's frustrating." Remember, empathy helps children feel accepted, understood, and leads to problem solving.

Step 2. Hand the problem back.

"What do you think you are going to do?" Don't be surprised if they shrug their shoulders and mumble, "I don't know."

Step 3. Get permission to share ideas.

Ask, "Would you like to hear what some other kids have tried?" Do not say, "Would you like to hear what I think you should do?" They might answer, "No, I don't want to hear what other kids have tried." That's okay. In that case simply reply, "Well, let me know if you change your mind."

Step 4. Provide a few ideas.

If the child is interested in hearing "what some other kids have tried", you have the green light to say:

Some kids decide to ____. How would that work for you?

This is your chance to share your most brilliant ideas. But don't give any hint that you think one idea is better than another. Let the child decide that. You might inspire your child to come up with some solutions on his own, and he might even choose *his* solution over your brilliant one.

When we add, "How would that work for you?" to each idea, the child is prompted to consider the consequence of each idea.

It might be good practice to start with a not-so-brilliant idea. Children tend to reject the first idea, so don't waste your brilliant idea on the first one.

Step 5. Allow the child to choose the solution.

Resist the urge to suggest which solution you think is best. Real learning comes from deciding on a solution, carrying out the solution, and experiencing the consequence. End by saying, "Does that help? If anybody can figure it out, you can. I'd love to hear how it turns out. If you need to talk anymore, just let me know."

Note: If the problem is too big or too dangerous for the child, then it would be wise for the parent to get involved in the solution. But there are plenty of other opportunities to hand the problem back to the child.

Here is an opportunity for a mother to teach her son how to solve a problem by giving the problem back to him.

Tommy raced into the house from the back yard. "Joey is calling me names," he cried.

Mom: "Hmmm. That must have hurt your feelings." **(Step 1)**

Tommy: "It did."

Mom: "What do you think you are going to do?" **(Step 2)**

Tommy: "What?"

Mom: "What do you think you are going to do?

Tommy: "I dunno."

Mom:" Would you like to hear what some other kids have tried?" **(Step 3)**

Tommy: "I guess."

96

Mom: "Some kids decide to call names back. How would that work for you?" **(Step 4)**

Tommy: "Not good. I tried that."

Mom: "Hmmm. Okay. Some kids decide to just ignore their friend. How would that work for you?"

Tommy: "I dunno."

Mom: "Hmmm. Okay. Some kids decide to play with another friend. How would that work for you?"

Tommy: "I dunno."

Mom: "Well, does that help? If anybody can figure it out, you can. I'd love to hear how it turns out. If you need to talk anymore, just let me know." **(Step 5)**

Can you think of any more options for Tommy to consider? Tommy's decision might be to do nothing. The important thing is that he was empowered to make that decision himself and learn from its consequence.

Let Kids Make Mistakes

Parents often consider mistakes to be a bad thing. They set high standards for their children, and when someone fails to meet those standards, the parents get angry. "No no no. Not that way. Haven't you listened to a thing I've said?" This causes a child to feel like a disappointment, inadequate, or a klutz. They will avoid taking risks and learning new things for fear of humiliation. They will be sneaky and try to hide their mistakes from unknowing parents. Parents who criticize their children for making mistakes take away from their sense of acceptance and belonging.

Some parents feel if they don't show disapproval or inflict shame or punishment, they are acting permissively and letting their children get away with something. There is a better way. It's not being controlling and it's not being permissive. It's helping children take responsibility for their mistakes and learning from them. Here's what you do.

First of all, realize that kids make mistakes. They just do. Often when they try something new, they fail. Sometimes they just do stupid things because they do not have the foresight or the knowledge to avoid trouble. Kids gain foresight and knowledge by learning from the poor choices they make. Secondly, consider mistakes as opportunities to learn. It is much easier for a child to take responsibility for a mistake if her parents see it as a learning opportunity rather than something bad.

Then you are going to lead your child in the following discussion using the "Three Whats":

1. **What happened?** Do not ask, "What were you thinking?" or "Why did you do that?" Asking "why" gives the child an opportunity to dodge responsibility by putting the blame on something or someone else.

2. **What needs to be made right?** Does anything need to be paid for, replaced, or repaired? Was anyone hurt physically or emotionally who deserves an apology.

3. **What might you do differently next time?** Do not say, "I hope you learned your lesson." Do not tell the child what she should have learned or what she should do next time. However, you can ask: "What might you do differently next time?"

Work on a solution together. "What do you think would happen if you were to try this...?"

Mistakes are going to happen so expect them and embrace them. Consider mistakes to be wonderful learning opportunities; opportunities to gain foresight, knowledge and empowerment. You may occasionally observe your child about to make a mistake and want to jump in and prevent it from happening to protect your child from failing and feeling hurt. If the mistake is not going to be dangerous to anything or anyone, consider allowing the child to make the mistake. A child will learn more from making a mistake than from any lecture or warning from you, because natural consequences are the best teachers. Naturally, if you know your child is about to make a dangerous mistake, you need to intervene to prevent it from happening.

If a child decides not to wear her helmet while on a bicycle, then you must step in and prevent that from happening. "Either you wear your helmet, or you don't ride." But if the child decides to ride her bike through a bunch of prickly weeds and gets a flat tire that will be a learning experience she won't forget. The upside for you is, you will get to teach her how to patch a flat tire.

When she makes a mistake, say, "That's okay." "What happened?" "What might you do differently next time?" Sometimes you won't even need to go through the Three Whats: "That's okay, try again," Will be all you need to say.

Dad had just purchased a new lawn mower. It was self-propelled, had plenty of power, and even had an electric starter. It was the nicest lawnmower he had ever owned. This was the third time he had used it to mow the lawn and his 12 year old daughter Nicole asked to take it for a spin. She easily maneuvered it around the front yard and then around the fire hydrant by the curb.

All of a sudden, BANG! The mower sputtered and stopped. Upon inspection of the crime scene, Nicole had come too close to the fire hydrant, causing the mower blade to hit one of the bolts coming up from the base of the fire hydrant. Not only had the lawn mower blade been damaged (which was replaceable) but the shaft from the engine to the blade was bent (a major and expensive repair). The lawn mower was inoperable. It had gone from being a shiny lawn mower to a shiny lawn ornament in a split second. "Dad, I'm so sorry," said Nicole.

Dad was speechless. He knew that whatever came out of his mouth in the next few seconds would be remembered forever by his now trembling daughter. He wanted to tell her how careless she was and that he felt disappointed in her. He wanted to tell her that he expected her to pay for the repairs and if it couldn't be repaired she was going to pay for a new lawn mower, and oh yeah, she was grounded for the rest of the summer.

Instead, he took a deep breath, exhaled and said in a calm voice, "What might you do differently next time?" Nicole, who was mentally preparing for dad to explode, was taken back. Careful not to make eye contact, she said timidly, "Stay away from the fire hydrant?" Dad stood there, silently, still in disbelief, looking at his new broken lawn mower. Then he wheeled the lawn mower away. Nothing more was said.

A month later the lawn mower was back from the repair shop, as good as new. "Let's take it for a spin," dad said to Nicole. "No thanks, dad." "Nonsense," said dad, grinning. "When you get bucked off you jump right back on, right? Come on. I trust you."

Nicole reluctantly followed her dad outside, and when invited to take the controls, she stayed far, far away from the curb and the fire hydrant. After the lawn was done, Nicole said to her dad, "Dad, you had every right to lay into me when I broke the lawn mower, but you didn't. Thank you." Dad just smiled, thinking how close he had come to damaging his relationship with his daughter.

I use the "Three Whats" on myself, whenever I make a mistake. I take comfort to know that no matter how badly I mess things up, if I try to make things right and learn from my mistakes, I'll be better off for having had the experience.

I sure made my share of mistakes as I learned new parenting principles. But I didn't give up. Every time I made a mistake I tried to determine what I would do differently next time. And there always seemed to be a next time. A home makes a good laboratory for experimenting.

You will be an inspiring example to your children when they see you make mistakes. Children learn accountability from parents who are models of accountability.

Chapter 9 - Principle #6 - Have Weekly Family Meetings

Even if your family is super busy, it is important to spend quality time together on a regular basis. This is a powerful principle that produces positive results. Once you experience the benefits, you will make it a high priority.

Call it "Family Meeting", "Family Time", "Family Council", or "Family Night". Whatever you call it, no other event will bring your family closer together. You will see how this family gathering incorporates all the principles we have looked at up to this point, and how it boosts everyone's sense of belonging and personal power. You'll also find they are quite fun.

Here's how it works. Once every week you gather everyone in the family together. Ideally, this should happen on the same day at the same time so everyone can come to expect it and schedule around it. Sunday evenings work well for many families. Some families find it best to do it on a week night.

Hold your Family Meeting where ever it is convenient, comfortable, and where there are as few distractions as possible. You may want to move the location from time to time for a little variety. The living room, kitchen, or backyard make good spots. Don't hold it during dinner. Make your Family Meetings separate from dinner.

Family Meetings don't need to take a long time. Depending on your agenda, it could be as short as 20 minutes or take up the entire evening.

What Do We Do?

A Family Meeting is a way for all family members to reconnect, give and receive compliments, update calendars, learn new things, solve problems, and have fun. Each Family Meeting will follow an agenda. The agenda is to help you cover all the important activities and stay on track, but it can be as flexible as you want. The activities are geared to include everyone's participation. Following are activities that will contribute to the success of your Family Meetings.

Appreciation Time

This is where everyone takes a minute to tell one thing they appreciated about each family member during the past week. This is the group version of looking for good behavior and rewarding it. The first time you do this, it might seem a little awkward to family members who are not used to giving or receiving compliments. But as you continue to do this every week, it won't be long before everyone will look forward to hearing something good about themselves – especially from their siblings. Mom might get the ball rolling by saying something like this:

"I appreciate dad for spending his lunch-hour last week to take Suzi to the dentist. That really helped me out. Aubrey, I noticed you made a real good effort to get all your homework done this past week. Good job. Keep up the good work. I appreciate Suzi for helping Allison find her shoes on that day we were in a hurry to get out of here. You helped both of us. And Allison, I appreciate you helping me fix dinner the other night. We had fun, didn't we?"

Then dad, Aubrey, Suzi and Allison will each take a turn and tell one thing they appreciate about each of the other family members. It only takes a few minutes and is a good way to set a positive tone for the rest of the meeting.

Calendar Time

Family Meetings are a good time to coordinate everyone's schedule for the following week. Bring the family calendar to the meeting and write down everything that needs to be remembered: dance lessons, basketball practice, school play rehearsals, school projects due, doctor appointments, etc. Decide who is going to take whom and at what time. Make sure that your next Family Meeting is scheduled on your family calendar. During the week, keep the calendar where everyone can see it.

This is also good training for children to keep their own calendars to keep track of events in their own lives like babysitting, sleep-overs, birthday parties, school assignments or anything they need to remember. They should bring their calendars to the Family Meeting.

This is the time to resolve scheduling conflicts, rather than finding out later that you need to be in two places at the same time. Calendar Time will help avoid forgetting important events, help everyone to get where they're supposed to be when they're supposed to be there, and eliminate chaos and anxiety.

Treat Time

Everyone enjoys treats, so be sure to make treat time part of every Family Meeting. But consider leaving Treat Time for the end of Family Meeting or to be included during Fun Time. That way everyone will have something to look forward to. Treats can be anything delicious: cookies, cake, pie, ice cream, brownies, or scones. (Or a new experimental recipe, maybe? Be adventurous). At your next family meeting, ask for suggestions.

Fun Time

When your children grow up and look back at past Family Meetings, the thing they will remember most (and talk about) will be the fun times that they shared together as a family. So make Fun Time a part of every Family Meeting. Fun Time will bond your family together. If you only have time to do one thing, do Fun Time. Fun time can be as simple as going around the room and having everyone tell a joke, to something more ambitious like going for a bike ride. It should be the last item on your Family Meeting agenda. Try board games, card games like Uno, or a skill game like Jenga. There are hundreds of fun games and activities for families. Here are some resources:

- Ask your kids for suggestions.

- Get ideas from another family who holds regular Family Meetings.

- Check out a book from the library about family activities.

- Do a Google search on "Activities for kids" or "Family Activities".

There are other things you can do to add value and variety to your Family Meetings. You can use Family Meetings for open discussion, to teach something, or to solve a problem. You can also invite a guest to attend or even invite a guest to give a presentation. After holding a few Family Meetings, you will find it beneficial to get the children involved by assigning Family Meeting roles (discussed below). The entire Family meeting should be enjoyable. Your number one goal should be to make Family Meetings a time that the whole family looks forward to.

Open Discussion

Open Discussion is the opportunity for anyone to talk about anything. It can be used to ask for help in making a decision, register a complaint, present a problem and find a solution, make an announcement, or request help with something. Aunt Millie is coming to visit us for three days. How can we prepare? We are going to be painting the downstairs. What daily routines will need to be changed? There is not enough hot water to go around in the morning. What can we do so everyone gets a hot shower? We have a vacation coming up. What are some activities we would like to do? Every family member is encouraged to offer input. Complaining and problem solving can sometimes get volatile, so set some rules:

- Let everyone know they are expected to use a calm voice.

- Only one person gets to speak at a time.

- Everyone will have a chance to offer their input.

- Use "I Feel" statements – as discussed in the chapter 13.

When it comes to problem solving, ask everyone to offer a possible solution. The solution should not be a result of a majority vote. Majority vote means there are winners and losers, and you should avoid making anyone feel like a loser. You want to work together to find a solution that everyone can get behind (or at least live with) for at least one week. Once the decision is made, give it a week to see how it works, and then bring it up for discussion in the next Family Meeting.

If possible, let the children come up with the solution that they are willing to try, even if you feel it is not the best solution. Sometimes the most effective training is to let children feel the consequences of their decisions and then make needed changes. Stress that what we decide as a family, we commit to as a family. This attitude will get everyone pulling together as a team. Solving problems together promotes family unity – even if the solution is not the best one. It is better to promote family unity than to have mom and dad dictate what they feel is the best solution.

At the next Family Meeting get everyone's opinion about how well the problem was solved. Do not say, "I told you so." Tweak the solution if needed and try it for another week. Once children get used to solving problems as a family, they will feel safe going to their siblings for opinions and advice. They will learn to solve problems among themselves.

Open Discussion is a great time to teach the skill of problem-solving. Group problem-solving involves various skills including listening, expressing one's point of view, understanding another person's point of view, creative thinking, coming up with possible solutions, analyzing possible consequences, and reaching consensus. Problem-solving is a skill that takes practice, and your Family Meetings will be a good training ground for that.

Teach Something

The weekly Family Meeting offers a good opportunity to teach. This is a good time for mom or dad to teach something that might be awkward or difficult under any other circumstance. This is where good values are discussed and learned. Consider announcing next week's topic and invite everyone to bring questions or comments they think of during the week.

Mom or dad can offer a short lesson, but lessons do not need to be restricted to them. After Family Meetings have become routine, each of the children should have an opportunity to teach something, depending on their age. Teaching is a good life-skill to have, and the Family Meeting is a good time to learn and practice. Additionally, the person who prepares and gives the lesson usually is the one who learns the most. You can assign someone a topic, or you can ask them to choose a topic they are interested in. Give them plenty of time to prepare and be there for them as a resource. You may want to team-teach so it is not so scary. Don't force anyone to give a lesson. Family Meetings are meant to be enjoyable.

Lessons don't need to be long. Depending on the subject and the age of the person giving the lesson, a lesson might be only a couple of minutes. Lessons should not be lectures or preaching. They should be more of a discussion: asking questions and getting

108

opinions. Some opinions you may not agree with. That's okay. Do not argue. Family Meeting lessons may lead to some serious one-on-one discussions with your children at a later time. Here are some possible topics. Share them with your family and ask them what they think should be added to the list.

How to give a lesson
What to do in case of a fire
Good table manners
How to greet people
How to solve problems
Using "I Feel" statements (explained in the chapter 13)
Stories of ancestors
Respect
Honesty and trust
Charity
Moral cleanliness
Peer pressure – what to do if offered drugs, etc.
Talking with strangers
Drinking and using drugs
Using tobacco
Being kind
Forgiveness
Sacrifice
Texting
Bullying
The importance of education
The importance of choosing good friends
Being a good friend
Gratitude
The importance of physical exercise

Healthy eating
Service to others
Dress, appearance and modesty
The language we use
How music affects us
Budgeting money
The importance of work

You might feel uncomfortable teaching some of these topics. But remember this. Your children will form opinions about all of these topics sometime during their early lives. Many of their opinions will be based on information they gleaned from the media (TV, movies, magazines, and the internet) and from people who are not concerned about their welfare. It will be easier for you to teach them before they are influenced by other sources. Changing their opinions after they have formed them can be a lot more difficult than helping to form their opinions. You need to help form their opinions and Family Meetings are the perfect place to do that.

Invite a Guest

Although most of your Family Meetings will involve only your family members, you can invite a guest to add a little variety to the gathering. Guests could come from extended family like grandparents, aunts, uncles, or cousins. Perhaps one of your children would like to include one of their friends in your Family Meeting. You could invite a friend or a neighbor to experience a Family Meeting. You could also invite an entire family to join you. Your Family Meeting might inspire others to start their own family meetings. Just make sure there are enough treats to go around.

What if your lesson or Fun Time was directed by a special guest? That would definitely add some variety and create some fun anticipation. Ask grandma to tell some stories about growing up in Ireland. Ask grandpa to tell some of his army stories. Ask Aunt Hazel, who is famous for her delicious bread to teach her secret recipe. Ask origami expert, Cousin Mike, to teach how to make a paper swan.

Don't think a guest speaker is limited to family members only. Do you have a friend or neighbor who would be good at teaching a lesson about drinking and using drugs, healthy eating, or budgeting money? Most people would feel flattered to be invited to teach something at your Family Meeting, and your kids might pay more attention to a guest speaker than to you.

Assign Roles

After your family has settled into the routine of having regular family meetings, give your children the opportunity to become more involved by assigning roles: Meeting Leader, Note Taker, Calendar Updater, Treat Server, Fun Time Planner, or Lesson Giver. All family members should have a role. Rotate roles each week so everyone has a chance to participate in a different role. This will enable everyone to get involved, have a say in family matters, and feel empowered.

There will be Bumps in the Road

Your aim should be to make Family Meetings enjoyable so that everyone will want to come back the next week. Make sure to have Fun Time at the end of every Family Meeting even if it's only for a few minutes – even if it's the only thing you have time for. With that said, be advised that all Family Meetings will not run smoothly. Some will be frustrating and some will be boring. One or more family members might come in a bad mood or be in a hurry to get somewhere. Arguments may erupt during your meeting.

Do not get discouraged. Adjust if you have to. Don't let Family Meeting go too long. Don't let one person dominate the discussion. Don't wander off the agenda for too long. Turn cell phones off – hey, it's only for a few minutes! Do not go a week without holding a Family Meeting. But if you do, just get back on track. You will find that Family Meetings are the best way to bring a family close together, and the best forum in which to teach problem-solving, decision-making and good family values. Some Family Meetings will be memorable, and some forgettable. Some will be outstanding, and some will be life-changing. The key is to keep trying.

Chapter 10 - Making Rules

One of the biggest frustrations parents have is the daily struggle to get their children to obey rules and expectations – to cooperate. The struggle occurs because parents care that their children are safe, clean, kind, helpful, and cooperative. But kids put exploring, having fun and feeling good at a higher priority. It seems the more parents try to get their children to cooperate, the more children resist. But kids need rules and boundaries. And they need to clearly understand what is expected of them before cooperation can happen.

The purpose of this chapter is to teach that rules must be understood before they can be enforced. Some rules don't need a lot of explaining, and some do. Problems occur when a child does not fully understand the rule.

If (I mean when) a child breaks a rule, then you will use techniques to enforce the rule, which will be covered from the next chapter on. But before you can enforce the rule, you must, of course, make the rule, and the child must understand it. There are three ways to make rules. As we move from one to the next, you will notice more emphasis is placed on helping the child understand the rule. Use the one you feel is best depending on the age of the child and the difficulty of the rule.

1. Quick and easy

2. Get the child to repeat the rule

3. Teach a skill

Quick and Easy

"Hey, no jumping on the couch!" is a quick and easy way of making a rule. Most rules are made on an as-needed basis, right? You don't know a rule is necessary until you see a need for it. "Take your shoes off before you walk on the carpet." "Ride your bike on the sidewalk, not in the street." "Eat your cookies in the kitchen." "Dirty clothes go in the laundry basket."

Rules made the quick and easy way, however, may not make a very big impression. Children can tune you out when you give them, conveniently forget them, consider them a one-time deal, or regard them as unimportant. They might even test those rules later to see if parents are serious about enforcing them. That's their job. Kids are good at dodging or finding loopholes in rules made the quick and easy way.

Get the Child to Repeat the Rule

You do this by getting the child's attention, explaining the rule, and having the child repeat the rule back to you. This will increase the chance that the child will understand and remember the new rule.

"Hey, no jumping on the couch! Come here. Couches are for sitting. Not for jumping. So I'm going to make a rule, no jumping on the couch. Can you remember that?" The answer will always be "yes." Kids can be pretty good at tuning you out and telling you what you want to hear. Then you'll say, "Okay, what's the rule?" They'll say, "umm, I forgot." You'll remind them, "The rule is, no jumping on the couch. So, what is the rule?" When they repeat the rule to your satisfaction, then you compliment (reward good behavior): "That is exactly right. Thank you."

Will you have to remind them again? Probably. "Hey." you say in your calm voice. "I see you jumping on the couch" In many cases, this is all you will need to say in order for them to remember the rule. No lecture is necessary. But if they appear to have forgotten, simply say, "We talked about this, remember? What's the rule?" Don't let them ignore you. Repeat if needed, "What's the rule?" They will look down and shrug their shoulders. "The rule is no jumping on the couch. What is the rule?" When they repeat the rule to your satisfaction, then you are done. "Good. That is exactly right." The child's self-esteem remains intact. Later, and this is important, look for good behavior and reward it: "I noticed you haven't jumped on the couch for a long time." Then give a fist-bump.

Here are the steps to this method:

1. Stop the behavior.

2. Teach what you expect.

3. Have the child repeat the rule to your satisfaction.

Teach a Skill

Some rules take a little more training; training that would resemble teaching life-skills. Watch how mom teaches this next rule:

"From now on I would like you to wash your hands by yourself when I call you for dinner. So I'm going to show you what I expect, okay? Come with me. First, put the stool in front of the sink. Very good. Now get on the stool and turn the hot and cold water on so it's warm. Go ahead and try. A little hotter. Great. Now get your hands wet. Good. Now, one squirt of soap. I want you to scrub your hands all over. Keep scrubbing and count to 10. Not so fast. Now rinse. Make sure all the soap is rinsed off. Nice job. What do you think you do now? That's right. Turn off the water. Now what? Dry them. Are we done? Not quite. One more thing to do. What is it? (pointing to the stool) That's right. Put the stool back where it goes. You got it. So what are you going to do when I call you for dinner? That's right, wash your hands. Do you know why I want you to wash your hands before dinner? Because dirty hands can make you sick. So, why do we wash our hands before dinner? That's exactly right. Good job."

To a parent, clean hands mean all the dirt goes down the drain. To a child clean hands could mean get my hands wet and wipe the dirt off on the towel. You cannot assume a child knows what clean hands mean without *teaching* what clean hands mean.

You'll notice that mom never said, "Do you understand?" A child will always respond "yes" to that question whether he understands or not. Mom had her child actually do everything she wanted her child to understand and remember. She had the child go through the motions of washing his hands, which teaches so much more than simply explaining. She also explained why this expectation was being set: because dirty hands can make you sick. She kept it very simple.

Now mom needs to enforce the rule. She will watch from a distance to see if her child follows her expectations. If the child forgets to wash, mom will calmly remind the child, "I see hands that are not washed."

If the child makes a good effort but does not do a good job at washing, let it go in the beginning. Do not expect perfection. Expect mistakes. This is not the time to criticize. What is important is that you look for good behavior, no matter how small, and reward it: "I noticed you went into the bathroom to wash your hands when I called you to come to dinner. Thank you." Never mind if the washing wasn't exactly as you taught. We want the child to feel good about whatever he did right. If more training is necessary, do it sometime before the next meal. "Hey. Let's practice washing our hands."

Don't forget, when a new expectation is set, always look for good behavior and reward it. "Let me see your hands. Hey, those are clean hands. Good job."

Teaching a skill requires more time than the other two methods. Some parents say they don't have the time. I suggest you can either spend time to teach, or spend time dealing with the same misbehavior again and again.

Even a household responsibility as simple as putting toys away deserves proper training. Don't say, "When I say, 'Time to clean up,' then you clean up. Do you understand?" That's not clear enough. Say something like, "When I ask you to clean up, you need to stand up right away, pick up a toy, put it in the toy box. Pick up another toy, put it in the toy box. And keep doing that until all the toys are picked up."

Demonstrate by putting toys in the toy box yourself. Then invite him to try it: "Let's practice. I'll ask you to clean up and you show me what you need to do.

Tommy, would you please clean up." Do the practice. This way Tommy understands by doing. And you can approve the way he does it or correct the way he does it by asking questions: "Is that a toy I see over there in the corner?" Make sure Tommy understands what the room should look like when the job is done: no toys on the floor – all toys in the toy box. "There, now nobody can step on any toys." Make sure the last thing you do is approve the way he does it. "You got it Tommy. That's exactly what I want you to do."

Some skills may require more time to learn. For instance, loading a dishwasher may require you and your child to load the dishwasher together for two or three days. You will teach which dishes go on the top rack and which dishes go on the bottom – and why, how to position the dishes on the racks, how to tell if a dish requires rinsing before loading, how to position the silverware and smaller items, what kind of soap to use, and how to start the dishwasher after it is loaded. Instead of criticizing, ask questions. "Is there any way to fit these last two dishes in there?"

Then you will invite your child to do it by himself, at which time you will exhibit superhuman patience and withhold criticism at all costs, because your child will do something different to make it his own unique way. It's a personal power thing. As long as the dishes are getting clean, don't sweat the small stuff.

Did you notice in the previous two examples that after the child was invited to try it, I advised against correcting the child with statements like, "You missed a toy over there," or "Move these bowls closer together to make room for a couple more dishes?" I suggested using a question instead: "Is that a toy I see over there in the corner?" "Is there any way to fit these last two dishes in there?" Questions encourage kids to think; to solve problems, and that will help them remember, and start them learning problem-solving skills. If you want to keep your children's attention and help them understand something important, ask questions. Questions also soften criticism, and when a child is learning something new, criticism can be discouraging.

Over time, your young apprentice will develop her own unique method for doing whatever it is you trained her to do. Don't criticize or correct just because it's not your way. If the job is getting done, it's all good. She is simply finding a positive sense of personal power by doing it her way.

Teaching Respect

Children cannot properly show respect if they do not know what respect is. A good time to teach respect is in your weekly Family Meeting. It might require more than one lesson and may continue to be a work in progress. Start by sitting down with your child, children, or family. Start by asking, "What is respect?"

You may have already trained your child in some forms of respect like saying please and thank you, and apologizing when necessary. So your questions might go something like this: "Is respect saying please and thank you?" You're looking for a "yes". "Is respect apologizing when you've hurt someone's feelings?" "Yes, that's right." "Does respect mean to always agree with someone?" "No. You can be respectful and not agree." "Does respect mean to be kind?" "That's right, it does." "Does respect mean to tease?" "No. That's right. Instead of teasing, what can we do?" "Be kind. That's right". "How does it make you feel when someone treats you with respect?" "Good. Yes. Me too." "How do you think others feel when you treat them with respect?" "Yes, they probably feel good too." "Do you think when you treat people with respect, that they will feel more like treating YOU with respect?"

Continue your discussion until you have come up with a short list of things that define respect. Resist the urge to criticize, argue or lecture. Remember, this is a work in progress. Children will learn respect over time by doing. Write the list on a white board or piece of paper. Better yet, have one of the children do the writing.

End the discussion with a challenge to practice being respectful to everyone over the next week and then plan to get together at the end of the week and talk about how things went; what went well and what didn't. During the week, try to catch your children being respectful and reward them: "I noticed that you said, 'Thank you'. That showed respect."

One of the best ways to reinforce the lesson you gave on respect is to set a good example. Treat others with respect – your spouse, your neighbors, strangers, and especially your children. Treat them with kindness. Apologize when necessary. Don't correct them in front of other people as that would embarrass them. Instead, ask to speak with them alone for a minute. Your children will be more likely to show respect for you and others if you respect them.

You should always be a good example of what you teach. If you set an expectation to rinse your dirty dish and put it in the dishwasher, you'd be wise to do the same. If the rule is to keep your bedroom clean, then you'd be wise to keep *your* bedroom clean too. If kids see you disobeying an expectation you established with them, they will feel justified in disobeying the expectation too.

The Problem with "Don't"

I want you to think about all the times you train your child by telling him what *not* to do. "Don't leave your dirty clothes on the floor." "Don't wander off." "Don't walk in the puddle." *"Don't"* can be confusing to a child. When you say "don't", your child has to decide on his own what it is he's supposed to *do*, and sometimes that's more thinking than he wants to do, so he ignores you. When you say, "Don't leave your dirty clothes on the floor," does that mean to throw them on the bed, under the bed, in a drawer, in the closet? "Wow. That's too much to think about. I'll just continue to throw them on the floor."

Also, when you tell your child don't do something, if gives him ideas about how to get your attention. When you say, "Don't touch your sister," deep in his subconscious mind he might be thinking, "Thanks for the idea, mom."

Remember back in chapter 4, I introduced the phrase: The behavior that receives the most attention is the behavior that will happen the most. If you focus on what *not* to do, your child will too, and that might be the behavior that will happen the most.

Let's get real. There are times when you have to say "don't". "Don't step in that puddle!" So go ahead and use "don't" sparingly, but when you can, follow it up with a "Do". "Don't step in that puddle! Walk around it." "Don't jump on the couch. Couches are for sitting." "Don't wander off. Stay close so we can talk to each other."

Stopping a Behavior

Let's make a rule that involves stopping a behavior. Hitting is a good example, but this example can be applied to other behaviors you'd like to stop, such as teasing, wandering off at the store, or running into the street. When the child is happy and calm, sit down with her and do some problem-solving.

Mom: "Jen, I know that your sister can be a real pain, and I know that sometimes you get so mad that you hit her. I want you not to hit her, no matter what she does, because there is no hitting in our home."

Jen: "But mom, she hits me first. Why don't you tell *her* to stop hitting?"

Mom: "I can see how that would make you mad, but still, no hitting."

Jen: "What if she hits me first? Then what?"

Mom: "What do you think you should do?"

Jen: "Hit her back."

Mom: "Would you like to hear what some other kids have tried?"

Jen: "What?"

Mom: "Some kids would decide to ignore her. How would that work for you?"

Jen: "Yeah, right."

Mom: "Some kids would go somewhere else to play. How would that work for you?"

Jen: "Whatever."

Mom: "Well, if anybody can figure it out, you can. I'd love to hear what you decide. If you need to talk anymore, just let me know."

You can't encourage cooperation or enforce rules unless you have set expectations. So if you're having a hard time getting kids to obey the rules, it might be that the children don't clearly understand. Teaching and problem-solving can lead to better understanding and cooperation.

Section 2 – Using Techniques

Responding to Unwanted Behavior

Chapter 11 – Enforcing Rules

"How do I get my kids to cooperate? I tell them to do something and they don't do it. I tell them *not* to do something and they do it. We have rules in this house, but they don't seem to care. I don't want to be a permissive parent and let them get away with everything, but some days I'm so exhausted from battling with them that I just let them have their way. Then I get so fed up with their misbehavior that I explode. I don't want to be that kind of parent. But I don't know what else to do."

Getting kids to cooperate depends more on the relationship you have built than on the techniques you use to deal with misbehavior. The better the relationship, the less need you will have for these techniques and the better these techniques will work. So it is important that you work on building a good relationship with your children. That's what all the chapters leading up to this one are about. If you read those chapters, and follow the recommendations, the relationships you have with your children will become dramatically better. Your children will feel included, accepted and loved. They well feel significant, and empowered. They will cooperate because they want to.

But kids will be kids, and even though children know what the rules are, they can choose to obey them or not, and sometimes they choose *not*. So from here on out we will focus on direct methods of correcting misbehavior.

Up until now we have focused on preventing bad behavior, and the suggestions in the chapters leading up to this one are recommended for every parent to do. However, from this chapter forward the focus will be on dealing directly with bad behavior, and the suggestions are for your consideration, to be used as you feel appropriate. So experiment. Try all the techniques and use those that feel and work best for you. Let's begin by looking at some words that invite children's cooperation. We will start with a simple, but effective technique called Describe What You See.

Describe What You See

Sometimes kids don't cooperate because they forget, get distracted or just don't think. Sometimes they don't cooperate because it's just not convenient. Sometimes they want to test you to see if *you* remember and are being consistent. In these cases, all you have to do is remind them. Here is a simple way to remind kids to remember a rule: describe what you see.

Rachelle is eating food where food is forbidden.
Describe what you see: "Rachelle, I see you eating food over the carpet."

Todd is playing when he should be doing his homework.
Describe what you see: "Todd, I see you not doing homework."

Jennifer leaves her coat on the floor.
Describe what you see: "Jennifer, I see your coat on the floor."

Mike does not put his dirty dishes in the dishwasher.

Describe what you see: "Mike, I see your dirty dishes still on the table."

No need for threats, commands, or lectures. Short, simple, and the child's self-esteem is left intact. It causes children to think, "You see my dirty dishes? What's up with that? Oh yeah, I'm supposed to put them in the sink." This technique also requires little time and effort on behalf of the parent.

Use One Word

Here is another short and simple way to remind kids about a rule. It requires very little effort but works like a charm. Kids also appreciate it because they don't get lectured. And sometimes less is more. The less you say, the better it works.

Rachelle is eating food where food is forbidden.
Use one word: "Rachelle. Food"

Todd is playing when he should be doing his homework.
Use one word: "Todd. Homework."

Jennifer leaves her coat on the floor.
Use one word: "Jennifer. Coat."

Mike does not put his dirty dishes in the dishwasher.
Use one word: "Mike, dishes"

Express How You Feel

When children break rules, it's okay to feel angry and it's okay to express that anger without feeling guilt or shame. It is possible to express your anger safely, respectfully, and in a way that says, "there is a limit to my patience".

Dr. Haim Ginott, in his book, *Between Parent and Child* [1], says, "In troublesome situations, parents are more effective when they state their own feelings and thoughts without attacking their child's personality and dignity. By starting with the pronoun 'I', parents can express their angry feelings and describe their child's disapproving behavior without being insulting or demeaning."

Here's the thing to remember. Feel free to express what you feel as long as you *do not attack the child's personality or character*. No insulting. No name-calling. No bringing up past grievances. Keep the focus on how *you* feel, why you feel that way, and what can be done in the future to make things better.

"Rachelle. I get real angry when you eat over the carpet. Food belongs in the kitchen!"

"Todd. It makes me mad when I see you playing when you are supposed to be doing your homework. When your homework is done, then you can play."

"Jennifer. I don't like it when I see your coat on the floor. Coats belong in the closet."

"Mike. I get so upset when you do not put your dirty dishes in the dishwasher because it makes more work for me. When all your dirty dishes are in the dishwasher, then you may leave the kitchen."

"When I see you hit your sister, I get angry. I can never allow you to hurt her."

"When I see toys and blocks and games scattered all over the floor, I feel like putting everything in a box and giving it all away. Either put your toys away when you are done playing with them, or I will take them away and you will not be able to play with them at all."

You can use the last three techniques in combination, and with increased intensity if needed:

Describe what you see: "Rachelle, I see you eating food over the carpet." Rachelle does not appear to be listening.

Use one word: "Rachelle, Food." Still, no response.

Express how you feel: "Rachelle. I get angry when you eat over the carpet. Food belongs in the kitchen! And it makes me just as mad when you ignore me. Now go."

Act, Don't Talk

I'm going to give you a replacement for begging, nagging, ordering, threatening, yelling, lecturing, and endlessly reminding. It is called "Act, Don't Talk". It means talk less and act more. Acting instead of talking communicates to your children that when you make a request, you mean business. When your kids know you mean business, they tend to cooperate willingly, even if they don't want to.

Do you ask your children to do something (or discontinue doing something) only to find that they ignore you? Then you ask again, followed by nagging or threatening or screaming. When you talk and don't act, children find it convenient to tune you out.

A mom takes her son to the park. Her son is playing in the sandbox with other children. He throws sand. "Don't throw sand," she says. He throws sand again. "I said don't throw sand." He throws sand again. "Do you want to go home? No throwing sand." He throws sand again. He is enjoying mom's attention. "I said no throwing sand. We'll go home, and I mean it."

You can see where this is going. Parents tend to ask, nag, and threaten, expecting with each request that their child will comply, but the child doesn't. Parenting by words alone does not always result in cooperation. This technique works best with smaller children.

Here's how it works. Ask only once and then take action. Here are some examples:

You take your son to the park. He is playing in the sandbox with other children. He throws sand. "Don't throw sand or we'll go home," you say. He throws sand again. You calmly walk over, take his hand and escort him home. Nothing more needs to be said.

Jane Nelsen, Ed.D., in her book *Positive Discipline A-Z*[2], says, "Over 75 percent of the problems parents have with young children would probably disappear if parents talked less and acted more. Children tune parents out because parents talk too much."

Two children are playing with a toy and get into a fight over it. "Play nicely," you say. They continue to fight. You quietly walk over, remove the toy and put it where they can't reach it. *You didn't need to say a word*. They know why you took it and they also know how to earn the privilege of getting it back. If they don't, you can tell them. I'll give the toy back after you've played nicely for a while."

Your daughter is squirting people with her squirt gun. You ask her to stop it. She continues. You walk over to her and hold out your hand. She looks at you as if to say, "What did I do?" You point the squirt gun and motion with your hand to give it to you. She gives you the squirt gun, and you walk away." No nagging. No arguing. And in this case, not one word spoken.

Your son is banging his fork on the table. You ask him to stop it. He continues. You take the fork away. No repeating your request.

Your daughter refuses to get into the tub. You pick her up and set her in the tub. No counting to three. No threatening to cancel her bedtime story. You ask her to get out of the tub. She ignores you. You pick her up and remove her from the tub.

You tell your son it's bed-time. He knows it's bedtime because you warned him 5 minutes ago that he has 5 minutes. He says, "Just a minute." You calmly take his hand and lead him to his bedroom.

Your daughter is running around the grocery store. You say, "Either stay by me, or you will ride in the cart. She persists in running around. You calmly pick her up and put her in the cart. The next day you are about to leave to go shopping. She asks:

"Where are you going?"
"Shopping."
"Can I come?"
"Not this time."
"Why not?"
"You tell me."
"Because I ran around last time?"
"Yup."

"I won't do it again, I promise."

"There will be other chances, but today, I'm going by myself."

Your family is eating at a restaurant and your son is being disruptive. You say, "If you can't sit down, we'll go sit in the car." He continues to be disruptive. Without another word you stand up and hold out your hand. "Do you want to walk or be carried?" He says, "I'll be good, I promise." You say, "Carried it is." He say, "No! I'll walk." You take him to the car. Luckily you had the foresight to come prepared with a wonderful book on CD, and your spouse has your meal boxed up for takeout.

The kids are fighting in the back of the car. You pull over to the side of the road and say, "We'll go when you are quiet and settled down." Then you pull out the murder-mystery book you've been reading and ignore the fighting.

It may take three of four times pulling over to the side of the road, or putting your daughter into the tub, or going home early from the park to convince your children that you mean what you say. But once you've done this *consistently* for a while, you should not have to "act" as often because the children will have learned from their behavior what will happen if they don't respond the first time you ask.

Remember to reward good behave when your kids have earned it: "Son, you stayed quietly in your seat through the entire meal. Thank you."

Grant a Fantasy

Use "grant a fantasy" when you cannot grant a reality. In Chapter 7, Principle #4 – Acknowledge Negative Feelings, we learned that children need to feel understood, and once they do, they feel better, and as a result, tend to behave better. We can use that same principle to motivate cooperation when a child wants something she cannot have. Use this technique when you have to tell a child "No." You will validate her feelings by granting her fantasy.

Lily was sitting down for breakfast. "I want frosty flakes, mom." I'm sorry honey, we're out." "But I want frosty flakes," Lily screamed as she started to kick her legs. "Honey, I wish I could give you the biggest bowl of frosty flakes you can imagine. A giant bowl. Would you want bananas or raisins on top?" "Both." "Both it is. And we'll top it off with some milk. Now, I have these two cereals. You choose. Which do you want? "Why should you grant a fantasy when you cannot grant a reality? Because in the small amount of time it takes to grant a fantasy, the child feels understood, and when the child feels understood, she tends to cooperate more. When we grant a child in fantasy what we cannot grant in reality, she is more able to deal with reality.

Billy and mom were at the toy store to select a gift for a birthday party. Mom turned around to see Billy holding a box containing a remote control car. "Mom." Billy said, "Can we buy this?" "That looks like fun." said mom. "You wish you could take that home." "Yeah, can we, mom?" "I wish I could buy that right now, but I can't." Billy, feeling disappointed, put the car back, but felt like mom understood how he felt.

Granting a fantasy works with adults too. Mom was admiring a dress at a clothing store. Dad approached her. Here are two different ways he could talk to her.

Way 1. "Don't even think about it. You know that's way out of our price range. You shouldn't even be looking at dresses like that. It only sets you up for disappointment."

Way 2: "I can see you in that dress. With the right accessories you would look pretty amazing. I would be proud to escort you anywhere."

Which way would get dad his favorite meal tonight?

Offer a Choice

In Chapter 2, Why Children Misbehave, you learned the two needs that every child tries to meet. One of those needs is the need to feel a sense of personal power. A sense of personal power means to feel significant, in charge of oneself, having the freedom to choose, to feel empowered. If a child does not feel a sense of personal power, she will go after it, and the easiest way to feel personal power is to simply say "no" to a request or command from a parent.

Choosing to obey is the one thing she has complete control over. When a parent says, "Go brush your teeth," the child can choose to exercise her personal power by saying, "No." When this happens the parent has a choice. He can demonstrate his "superior" strength by demanding, threatening, raising his voice, or physically taking his daughter to the bathroom – where she can still refuse to obey.

The alternative is to give the child a choice. One of the ways to feel a sense of personal power is to have the freedom to choose. If the father gives his daughter a choice, she can still achieve a sense of personal power without saying "no". "Would you like to brush your teeth in the bathroom or the kitchen?" Give this technique a try and see if it doesn't make a difference.

Problem-Solve Together

With this technique, parents work with their children to come up with a solution to a problem. Although this technique can be used to work out any disagreement, it works well on issues with behavior. You can also use this model for solving problems that are brought up in family meetings. This is a variation to the problem-solving method that was introduced in Chapter 8. You can still use the other method. I offer this method because it might meet your needs better. You can decide. There are three steps to this method:

1. Find out how the child feels about the behavior in question

2. Identify the problems the behavior causes

2. Talk about solutions

Step 1 - Find out How the Child Feels about the Behavior in Question

First identify the behavior you want to talk about and then get your child's opinion on the matter. "I notice the dishes aren't getting done when it's your turn and I'm thinking it's probably because you hate to do them." "You're teacher tells me that you are having a hard time completing your homework."

At this point your child may launch his defense. If he remains quiet, ask: "How do you feel about that?" Then listen. We've learned that only after a child believes that you understand what he or she is feeling, does that child care at all about listening to what YOU want to say. Use the skills you learned in Chapter 7, Principle #4 – Acknowledge Negative Feelings.

Step 2- Identify the Problems the Behavior Causes

Step 2 is to ask, "What problems do you think that might cause?" or "What problems do you think it causes when you don't do your dishes when it's your turn?" After the child takes his turn, it's your turn. "Do you think it might cause some bad feelings for the person who does dishes after you?" "Do you think it might cause some bad feeling for someone who wants to use a dish that hasn't been washed?"

Step 3- Talk About Solutions

Step 3 is to ask, "What suggestions do you have to solve this problem?" Be prepared to write all suggestions down. "Let's make a list of possible solutions." Don't prejudge or evaluate any suggestions at this point. You might be surprised to find that your child will come up with possible solutions that you haven't thought of.

After you have listed all possible solutions, go through the list together and eliminate those that would not work for whatever reason. "Now let's go through the list and decide what we want to keep and what we want to toss out."

"Can we talk?" dad said as he knocked on Tommy's bedroom door. "What can I do for you? I'm kind of in the middle of something," said Tommy." "Okay, then I'll get right to it." Dad said. "I notice the dishes aren't getting done when it's your turn and I'm thinking it's probably because you hate to do them." "Dad, I hate it when I have to empty the dishwasher, I hate to wash the pots and pans after the food has dried on them. I hate having to bring dishes over from the table, I hate having to scrape other people's plates, and I hate putting food away."

"Wow," said dad, "I had no idea. That must be totally overwhelming." "Yeah," said Tommy. "It's easier to not do them and get in trouble than do them and be mad the whole time." "I can see how that would make you mad," said dad. "On the other hand, it does create some problems, like doubling the work for the next person in line to do dishes, or making clean dishes unavailable for the next meal. Do you think together we could find a solution to this problem?" Dad and Tommy made a list of possible solutions:

1. Take Tommy off dishes duty.

2. Create a new job on the job chart for emptying the dishwasher.

3. Ask whoever is cooking, to rinse the pots and pans after using them.

4. Ask everyone to bring their plates from the table, scrape them into the garbage, and rinse them in the sink.

5. Ask everyone to help put all the food away after each meal.

This is the end of the story. I'll let you guess which possible solutions they kept and which they scratched off. Can you add anything to the list? Can your children?

Give Advance Warning

If the child is in the middle of doing something she enjoys and you are going to require that she stop and do something else, give some advance warning: "Susan, we're going to leave in 10 minutes." "Mary, bedtime in 5 minutes." Then when you say, "Alright, time to go," or "time for bed," the child is likely to "rebel less" because she has been expecting that she will have to stop.

Here is a variation to this technique that gives you an opportunity to offer a choice. Instead of informing the child that you have to leave in 10 minutes, offer a choice: "We need to go. Do you want to leave right now, or in 10 minutes?" "Do you want to go to bed now, or in 5 minutes?" This way, the child is informed and feels empowered at the same time.

Cooling-Off Period

Sometimes one of your children will do something that really sends you over the edge, causing your blood to boil and steam to come out of your ears. When emotions run high, you tend to say hurtful things, make rash decisions, and impose extreme punishments even when you know better. It's a natural reaction.

In situations like this it is better to take a time-out to put some distance between you and your child and allow some time to calm down and think rationally. Ask your child to go to his room. There is no need to restrict his activities once he is in his room, nor make him stay in his room for a specified amount of time, as this is not a punishment, but a time for you and him to cool off.

There is no need to feel that you must address the misbehavior immediately. It is better to postpone communication between the two of you for a while rather than run the risk of saying something that you will regret later. So go to that happy place in your mind and hang out there while you regroup. Then, when your blood pressure has returned to normal and you can think clearly, come together with your child to work on solving the problem. You might decide that a rule needs to be made, as described in the last chapter. Or perhaps you'll find it useful to use "I feel" statements or set consequences, both of which will be explained in upcoming chapters. Use the listening skills you learned about in Chapter 7, Acknowledge Negative Feelings.

Chapter 12 – When-Then Statements

In her book, *If I Have to Tell You One More Time*[1], Amy McCready describes a technique she calls "When-Then". This technique minimizes back-talk, whining, and complaining, and works on kids of all ages, 2 ½ years old and up – even teenagers.

See if this scenario sounds familiar. You ask your daughter to do something. She says, "It's not my turn." or "I did it yesterday." Or she ignores you altogether. You find yourself reminding, arguing, and justifying why she has to do it. Then you add a threat like no cell phone for the rest of the week. You know you always give in when you make that threat and you think, "I could do it easier and quicker myself," but you are sick and tired of doing what you asked her to do, so you resort to what has worked in the past. You yell. You don't want to but it seems to be the only thing that works. She finally starts to do what you asked her to do. Now you feel guilty for yelling and wonder if there is a better way. This technique could be the better way.

The main concept behind When-Then is to delay or deny a normally occurring privilege until the undesirable task has been completed. "No longer will you have to listen to, "Do I have to?" or "It's not fair!" It shuts down any chance of an argument. Here's how it works:

Ben: "I'm going over to Jack's."
Mom: "Are your chores done?"
Ben: "I'll do them as soon as I get back. I promise."
Mom: "**When** your chores are done, and done to my satisfaction, **then** you can go over to Jack's."

140

Ben:" But mom…"
Mom: Calmly walks away.

Mom walked away so Ben had no one to argue with. He now has a choice. He can do his chores and go to Jack's or not do his chores and not go to Jack's. Here are the steps to When-Then statements:

1. Develop the "When." This is the task you want your child to complete: empty the dishwasher, walk the dog.

2. Develop the "Then." Think of a normally occurring privilege that your child *wants* to do that you can postpone until the task has been completed. It should be something close to the time the task needs be completed. "When your hands are washed, then you can have a cookie." Getting the cookie is the obvious privilege in this case.

3. Say your When-Then statement in a calm voice. When you first start using this technique, emphasize the words WHEN and THEN. "WHEN you finish folding your clothes and putting them away, THEN you can use the computer." After you've used this technique for a while your children will come to understand that when you start a request with "when", you mean business and there's no point in arguing.

4. After you say the When-Then statement, you have to disengage and walk away. If you don't, the child will try to explain his way out of doing the task until you give in or get mad. If you find

it necessary to stay in the room, completely ignore the child's complaining. When you walk away or totally ignore the complaining, it sends a message that this matter is not up for negotiation. It also sends the message that you have complete confidence that your child will get the task done.

5. Don't give in. This is very important. If you say, "When your chores are finished, then we'll leave for soccer practice," stay firm. If it's time to go to soccer practice and his jobs aren't finished, then you must follow through and delay going until the jobs are done. This won't happen often. He'll soon come to know that when you say something, you really mean it.

Here are some examples of When-Then statements:

When you clean up your toys, **then** you can watch your show.

When you unload the dishwasher, **then** you can go outside and play with your friends.

When you've finished your homework and I've checked it, **then** we can leave for football practice.

When you've finished your family jobs, **then** you can facebook with your friends.

When you wash your hands, **then** you may eat.

When you stop whining, **then** I will listen to you.

When your dishes are in the dishwasher, **then** you may have desert.

When you put your helmet on, **then** you may ride your bike.

Set Up a Bedtime Routine

Use a When-Then statement to set up a bedtime routine that will happen regularly every night. This is a good way to get kids into bed without nagging and reminding. Your When-Then statement will include a deadline: "When your teeth are brushed and your pajamas are on, then we can read bedtime stories. But at 9:00, lights out." If the kids are ready for bed at 8:50, they get 10 minutes of bedtime stories. Ready at 8:59 means one minute of bedtime stories. After that, lights out.

In order for kids to get the sleep they need, try to keep bedtime consistent every night of the week. If bedtime is at 9:00, stick to that time every night. For children too young to tell time, use a timer to let them know that bedtime is when the timer goes off, and story time is over. If you are consistent and make bedtime a routine, you will have less trouble getting your kids into bed and less trouble getting them up in the morning.

Set Up a Morning Routine

Use a When-Then statement to set up a morning routine that will happen regularly every morning before school. After your kids have completed all of the "When" tasks, then they can enjoy a normally occurring privilege until they have to leave for school. Your When-Then could go something like this: "When you are dressed, your hair is brushed, your bed is made, your lunch is in your lunch box, your backpack is by the door, and your hands are washed, then you may eat breakfast. The kitchen, however, closes at 7:45 so you can get to the school bus on time."

Your child may have to go to school without having eaten breakfast, but after the first time, it will likely not happen again. If breakfast is not something your child gets excited over, choose another appropriate "Then", such as morning playtime, computer time, or TV time. Consider making a list of tasks that need to be accomplished each morning, and displaying it where everyone can see it. WHEN everything on the list is done, THEN you can Facebook.

The night before you start your first When-Then morning routine, sit down with your children and explain how the morning is going to unfold. Use your When-Then statement. Explain how they can expect the same routine every school morning. Soon your When-Then routine will become a routine and you won't have to remind your children anymore.

When-Then Tips

Make sure to use "when" and not "if". "If" sounds like a bribe, and it implies you are not confident the child will get the job done.

After saying your When-Then statement, you don't need to give reminders. But if the child does not do the "when," then you must deny the privilege. This may be hard on you, but you must remain firm if your child is going to take you seriously.

If you cannot think of a normally occurring privilege to go with your "then," choose another technique. Avoid denying a privilege that is not timely, such as: "When you clean your room then you can go to the birthday party tomorrow afternoon. In a case like this, you would be better off saying, "Son, I noticed your room needs to be cleaned and I also know that tomorrow you're planning to go to a birthday party. I'd like your room to be clean before you go, okay?" Then when your child says to you, "Bye, I'm going to the party," you can say, "WHEN your room is clean, THEN you can go to the party."

Chapter 13 – "I Feel" Statements

This technique was introduced briefly in Chapter 11. "I Feel" Statements let you express yourself in a respectful, but assertive manner without attacking or blaming the other person. Attacking or blaming puts others on the defense and is not an effective way to change someone's behavior. Using "I Feel" statements is a much more effective way to change someone's behavior. You can use "I Feel" statements with your children. You can teach your children to use "I Feel" statements with you, with their siblings, and with their friends. It takes a little practice, but it will be well worth it. You can use "I Feel" statements to talk about a behavior whether a rule surrounding the behavior has been made or not.

When addressing a behavior that needs to be changed, it is common for a parent to say something like, "You always leave your bike in the driveway," or "You never put tools away after you use them," or "You make me mad when you wear my clothes without asking." Beginning a statement with "You..." as in "you always", "you never" or "you make me" causes children to go on the defensive and argue instead of being receptive to your point of view. There are four parts to an "I Feel" statement:

1. "I feel _____" (state the *emotion* you are feeling: upset, mad, annoyed, disrespected)

2. "when you _____" (describe their behavior: forget to..., leave your...)

3. "because ____" (explain why their behavior causes you to feel this way - optional)

4. "I want ____" (state your request: I want... would you please... I would appreciate it if... and end with an agreement: "Can you do that?")

So instead of saying, "You always leave your bike in the driveway," you would say, "<u>I feel</u> upset <u>when you</u> leave your bike in the driveway <u>because</u> I have to get out of the car to move it. I'm also afraid I might not see it one day and run over it. <u>I want</u> you to make sure your bike is on the lawn or somewhere else before I get home from work. Can you do that?"

Instead of saying, "You never put my tools back when you're done using them." you would say, "<u>I feel</u> frustrated and mad <u>when you</u> don't put my tools back <u>because</u> I have to go looking for them. <u>I would really appreciate it</u> if you would put tools away when you are done using them. Okay?"

Instead of saying, "You make me mad when you wear my clothes without asking." you would say, "<u>I feel</u> mad and disrespected <u>when you</u> wear my clothes without asking. <u>Would you please</u> ask before you take them?" Notice that the "because..." step was left out. It's not always necessary if the reason is obvious.

When you put the emphasis on what *you* are feeling, rather than on the child, you can express everything you need to say without accusing, criticizing or attacking. Here are three more examples:

"<u>I feel</u> angry <u>when you</u> leave your dishes in the sink instead of putting them in the dishwasher <u>because</u> I shouldn't have to clean up after you. <u>I need you to</u> put your dishes in the dishwasher. Do you think you can do that?"

"Every afternoon I pick you up after school. I don't mind doing that. In fact, I enjoy seeing you. But I feel frustrated when I have to wait a long time for you to come to the car. So what I want you to do tomorrow and every day after that, is to be out to the car by 3:15. Can you do that for me?

Last one:

"I feel unappreciated when I take you places and you forget to say thank you. I need to hear a thank you. Will you please thank people when they do something for you?"

As always, be on the lookout for good behavior and reward it. When your child shows up to the car on time or thanks you for the ride, give a reward: "Thank you for being on time." "Thank you for thanking me for the ride."

Chapter 14 – Sibling Rivalry

There are two reasons that siblings fight: 1) Their need for a sense of belonging, and 2) their need for a sense of personal power. Does that surprise you?

The most common cause of sibling rivalry, according to child behavior experts, is a child's desire for the *exclusive* love and attention of his parents. A child will compete for his parent's love and attention the moment he realizes that he is starting to lose it to a brother or sister. We've talked about how every child has a need to feel a sense of belonging, and how he tries to satisfy that need by seeking attention. If receiving attention is threatened by another sibling, he feels he must compete for it, and does so by teasing and fighting. We call this Sibling Rivalry, but it can also be called competition for mom and dads' attention.

The second cause of sibling rivalry is a child's need to feel superior, in charge, or empowered. If parents are not helping to meet a child's need for a sense of personal power in positive ways, she will seek after it in negative ways such as teasing, bullying, or tormenting a brother or sister.

The 6 Principles discussed in chapters 4 through 9 will go a long way toward helping parents meet their children's basic needs of belonging and personal power in positive ways, thus reducing sibling rivalry.

Sometimes parents unintentionally promote sibling rivalry by doing the following:

- Give more attention to one child than another, or play favorites

- Make a child share his possessions (toys or whatever)

- Label a child: "Becki is the artistic one in the family"

- Compare children: "Jimmy, if you would just apply yourself more like Becki does..."

- Asking kids to compete: "Let's see who can clean their room the fastest."

It's understandable to feel that the aggressor, in a sibling dispute, should not get away with bad behavior and that the victim should be made to feel better, but it's also important to remember that the home is where kids should learn to solve problems. After they have moved out, you don't want them running to you every time they get into a disagreement or get their feeling hurt. So for those occasions when kids do lock horns, I'm going to provide you with some techniques to use. Here are three levels of sibling conflict with a recommended response for each.

Level 1. Siblings are disagreeing or arguing.

Intervention is not needed. Ignore. Let the children work it out themselves.

Level 2. Siblings are shouting. The situation is heating up.

Intervention would be helpful.

Step 1. Stop the fighting and acknowledge their anger: "Hold it, you guys! You two sound really mad at each other."

Step 2. Find out what's going on. "What's going on? Andrea, you first, then, when she's done, Kimmie, I want to hear from you." Give each child a chance to express her point of view without interruption from you OR the other child – whether what she says is true or not.

Step 3. Reflect the point of view from each child. "So Andrea, you want to play by yourself without Kimmie tagging along. Kimmie, you have nothing to do, so you want to play with Andrea."

Step 4. Summarize the problem. "That's a tough one. One of you wants to be left alone, and the other wants to play together."

Step 5. Express confidence that the two of them can work it out. "I'm confident that the two of you will come up with a solution *that is fair for both of you.*" Then if you feel inclined, you can make a suggestion: "One solution might be to arrange a time to play together later today. You decide." Then leave the room.

Level 3. Physical harm has happened or is imminent, or something has or is about to get broken.

The situation demands your attention. You must separate the children. Consider these two options:

Option 1: Say, "I won't permit hurting one another. We need a cooling-off period. You. Go to your room. And you, go to yours."

Option 2: Say, "I'm going to do something that one of you may not like. Kimmie, come with me and keep me company."

Sometimes you can't just ignore your children's squabbles and expect them to figure out what to do on their own. You need to train them. As with many expectations, this will probably require more than one training session. So, when everyone is calm, perhaps at your weekly Family Meeting (see Chapter 9) come together and train your children how to handle disagreements. Consider covering the following points:

- As for play-wrestling, decide on a word or phrase that one child can say during play-wrestling that will let the other child know that it is time to stop. A phrase like "stop now" lets the aggressor know that it is time to stop. However, a child who seeks a sense of personal power through wrestling or bullying will be slow to obey that rule. Chapters 4 through 9 show how to give children a sense of personal power in positive ways so they do not desire to seek it in negative ways.

- Teach what causes bad feelings and to avoid them: name-calling, endless teasing, hitting, pushing, taking toys without asking, tattling, and arguing. Ask the children, they'll tell you.

- Teach that either party can choose to walk away from a fight and put an end to it right then and there, and that good things come to those who patiently wait. For example, "He'll get tired of jumping on the trampoline after a while and you'll be able to have it all to yourself."

- Teach the benefit of taking turns: "If you'll let me play with it for 10 minutes, then you can have it for 10 minutes and we'll take turns."

- Teach when, and how to use "I feel" statements as described in chapter 13.

- Teach how to make respectful requests rather than making demands or just taking what you want. Teach how saying "please" and "thank you" can go a long way in getting what you want. "Please may I have my toy back?"

- Teach that if you want something someone else has, try trading something for it.

Earlier we learned two important principles: 1) the behavior that receives the most attention is the behavior that will happen the most (Chapter 4), and 2) the behavior that does not get any attention is the behavior that will go away (Chapter 5). So, in keeping with those principles, you are going to ignore annoying behavior by staying out of sibling squabbles, and reward good behavior when you see your children working to solve their own problems.

When fighting erupts, quickly and quietly leave the room, or if fighting happens in another room, don't go in. Although you appear to be ignoring the commotion, you will be discreetly listening in for three reasons:

1. to determine if the fight turns into a level 2 or a level 3 and you need to get involved.

2. to determine what training you may need to go over later.

3. to look for behavior that can be rewarded. "Hey you guys, I noticed earlier that you solved a problem together. Jimmy, you didn't scream or hit. Nice going. And Becki, you asked nicely. Good job." Remember to complement *each* child for doing something worthy of a compliment.

If kids come running to you with complaints about a sibling, you can listen to them and acknowledge their negative feelings as described in Chapter 7 – Principle #4, Acknowledge Negative Feelings. By doing so, you will give your children the freedom to solve their own problems and many times they will.

Teach Problem-Solving

There is another option to be considered when a sibling battle reaches level 2 or 3 and you feel you need to get involved. Your role will be that of a facilitator. You will not decide who is right and who is wrong, who should be reprimanded and who should be soothed. Your new role is to facilitate a conversation between siblings that will put an end to the problem by following these three steps:

1. **Acknowledge feelings**. In chapter 7, you learned how to respond to negative feelings. This is an excellent opportunity to practice what you learned. The first thing to do is identify the emotion each child is feeling and put it into a sentence: "Hold it you guys. Stop. Wait a minute. Jimmy, you seem really angry. Becki, you seem

really mad." Validating someone's feelings is a good way to start the problem-solving process without putting anyone on the defensive.

2. **Listen to each story.** Allow each of the children to tell their side of the story even if you were watching and you know what happened. It's important for each child to feel his or her story has been heard. But tell the children you want only the facts. "He's a stupid idiot" is an opinion, not a fact. "Okay, I want you to both tell me what happened, but I only want to hear what happened. I don't want to hear any blaming or name calling." As each tells his or her story, give your full attention to listening. Show that you are listening with "Oh", "Mmm", "I see" or nodding. Don't worry about who is right or whether or not they are telling the truth. That's not the facilitator's job. If you have taught your children about using "I Feel" statements, this would be a good time to suggest they use them.

3. **Ask for solutions.** After each child has explained the problem from their point of view, you will say something that will stun both of them because they are so used to you settling arguments. You will say, "Tell me some ideas that will solve this problem." Then remain quiet and see what happens. Allow only possible solutions to be given. No blaming or name calling. Someone may say, "But he started it." to which you will reply, "but what can you think of that might solve this problem?" With any luck, someone will come up with a solution they both

can live with and you will be done. However, if both shrug their shoulders and look at their shoes, try making a few suggestions in the form of a question. "What would happen if we took turns holding the baby, or what if everybody leaves the baby alone for a while?" Try to offer more than one solution to give them an opportunity to reach an agreement together.

What happens if you did everything a good mediator can do and the children still cannot reach an agreement. Then it's time to apply some motivation by using an Either-Or statement. "Either you both work it out or I'll take the baby and neither of you will get to hold him." "Either you find a way so you can both play with the blocks or we will put them away for the rest of the day." "Either decide on a movie you can both watch, or there won't be any movie." This will take the focus off arguing and put the focus on problem solving.

You might feel inclined to jump right into using the Either-Or technique and skip all the mediator stuff, but then your kids would miss out on the valuable problem solving training. They would also miss out on the possible solutions you suggest, and end up with no solutions from which to choose.

In their bestselling book, *Siblings without Rivalry*[1], authors Adele Faber and Elaine Mazlish describe how quickly parents should get in and out of sibling fights. They say, "Basically we try not to interfere, but when we must step in, it's always with the thought that at the earliest possible moment we want to turn the children back to dealing with each other. That's the best preparation we can give them for the rest of their lives."

By teaching your children how to solve problems between themselves and staying out of their fights, you empower them to figure things out on their own, a skill they will use the rest of their lives. It also releases you from the burden of having to be a judge and jury for every sibling argument.

Here's one more suggestion. Just like adults, sometimes kids need time by themselves. Make arrangements so that each child can occasionally have their own space and time to play with toys, by themselves or with a friend, without a sibling tagging along and without having to share with anyone.

Chapter 15 – Consequences

We learn from our mistakes. Another way to put that is, *we learn from the consequences that result from making poor choices.* The lessons we learn from consequences are more powerful than any lecture or punishment.

Consequences and punishment are not the same. Where consequences provide learning experiences, punishment promotes anger and resentment. There are two types of consequences, natural consequences and logical consequences.

Natural consequences are results of choices we make without intervention from anyone else. For example, forgetting to put ice cream in the freezer results in melted ice cream. Staying too long in the sun results in a sunburn. Eating too much candy results in a stomach ache. As adults, we experience a natural consequence *every time* we make a choice. Natural consequences can be positive or negative depending on the choices we make.

Kids make choices too. Poor choices result in negative consequences. So parents spend a good deal of time trying to keep their kids from making poor choices that they know would result in negative consequences: "Stay out of the street," "Stay away from the pool," "don't touch the burner on the stove," "Eat breakfast," "Don't forget your lunch," "Do your homework." Each rule has a negative, undesirable consequence if not followed.

Natural consequences are powerful ways to learn, but allowing children to learn from natural consequences is not always practical. You tell your children to stay out of the street because the natural consequence is to be hit by a car. You teach them to brush their teeth or they will experience cavities. You instruct them to stay close to you at the store or they might get lost. But children do not have the foresight nor the knowledge to avoid making poor choices that could result in unacceptable natural consequences. Introducing logical consequences; consequences that parents provide to replace the unacceptable natural consequences.

Logical consequences can be positive or negative. Children behave well to enjoy the positive consequences of behaving well. Rewarding good behavior, as discussed in chapter 4, is all about providing positive logical consequences. Negative logical consequences are substitutes for negative natural consequences with the intent of preventing the natural consequence from ever happening.

The natural consequence of not brushing teeth is getting cavities. Since you don't want your children to experience this natural consequence, you make a rule and substitute the natural consequence with a logical consequence: "Kids, I'm concerned about your teeth. I don't want you to get cavities and I know that brushing teeth helps prevent cavities. I want you to brush your teeth every night before bed. I also know that sweets like candy and desserts help give you cavities. So, if you do not brush your teeth every night before bed, there will be no sweets; no candy, no desserts, no treats of any kind. Now, just so I know you understand, can you please tell me what I just said?"

No need to remind the kids after that. The next day, have a chocolate pie for dessert. "Okay, you may have a piece if you brushed your teeth last night. Mom, I saw you brush your teeth, Jenny, I saw you brush your teeth, Sam? Oh, that's sad. You didn't brush your teeth last night." Say no more. Let the consequence do the teaching. Do not let Sam's tears make you cave in. Tomorrow night, have chocolate chip cookies.

The good thing about logical consequences is that you usually have to enforce the consequence only once or twice before the child decides to consistently obey the rule. The consequence does all the teaching so you don't have to. You *do not* have to say anything like, "See? I told you what would happen, didn't I?" or "I hope you learned your lesson." Here are the steps to making consequences work best:

1. **Make the rule.**

This was addressed in Chapter 10, Making Rules. At the time the rule was made, it had no consequence attached. You hoped the child would obey the rule with only a little reminding. But that has not been the case. The child continues to disobey the rule.

2. **Develop the consequence**.

First, determine the *natural* consequence. Would the natural consequence be the appropriate consequence? Perhaps going without lunch because the child forgot to take it would be an appropriate natural consequence. If a natural consequence is not appropriate, then decide on a logical consequence. The logical consequence should be related to the rule if possible. It should also be reasonable (not too harsh). If you cannot think of a logical consequence then don't use this technique. Use another technique or do more training as explained in chapter 8, Teach Life Skills. Following is a list of rules, along with their associated natural consequences and logical consequences. Notice that for some rules, the natural consequence is the best and only choice.

Rule: Wear your bicycle helmet.

Natural Consequence: Or you might fall and hurt your head.

Logical Consequence: Or you lose the privilege of riding your bike.

Rule: Stay next to me at the supermarket.

Natural Consequence: Or you might get lost or hurt.

Logical Consequence: Or you will ride in the shopping cart, wait in the car with an adult, or immediately go home and not be invited to come next time.

Rule: Do not go near the pool.

Natural Consequence: Or you might fall in and drown.

Logical Consequence: Or you will stay inside.

Rule: Do your homework.

Natural Consequence: Or you will get bad grades and be stuck with a poor job.

Logical Consequence: Or you don't go anywhere or do anything until it's done and I check it.

Rule: Don't leave your bike on the driveway.

Natural Consequence: Or mom or dad will have to get out of the car to move it before parking in the garage and it might get run over.

Logical Consequence: Or you lose your bike-riding privileges.

Rule: You have a half hour to clean your room.

Natural Consequence: Messy rooms are stinky and unsightly. Your child's home will likely be cluttered and unorganized.

Logical Consequence: Or I will put everything left out, in a box and the box will be unavailable for one week.

Rule: Your chore is to fill and start the dishwasher.

Natural Consequence: Or dishes pile up, the kitchen will look like a mess, and there will be no clean dishes to eat with.

Logical Consequence: Or you will not go anywhere or play games or watch TV until you've done your job.

Rule: Give yourself enough time to eat breakfast.

Natural Consequence: Or you will be hungry until lunch.

Logical Consequence: None.

Rule: Remember to take your lunch.

Natural Consequence: Or you will be hungry until snack-time or dinner.

Logical Consequence: None.

Rule: Don't tip over your glass of milk.

Natural Consequence: Or you will have to clean it up.

Logical Consequence: None.

Rule: Sit still in your seat while we are at a restaurant.

Natural Consequence: Or you will disturb other customers and anger the restaurant staff.

Logical Consequence: Or you will wait in the car with a parent until everyone else gets done eating.

3. **Explain the consequence.**

Sit down with your child or children and explain the rule and the consequence attached.

4. **Follow through with the consequence.**

The nice thing about consequences is that you can take action when a rule is broken without having to explain anything. You have taught your child the rule and the consequence. If the rule is broken, calmly implement the consequence that you and your children have talked about. If your child throws a tantrum, ignore it and walk away (as long as the child is in a safe place). You do not need to remind your child to obey the rule. Let the consequence do the teaching. Your child will soon come to realize that when you say something, you really mean it, and if the child breaks the rule, the consequence is certain to follow. When you catch your child obeying the rule, don't forget to reward the good behavior.

Here is an example of a father adding a consequence to a rule. The son is dribbling his basketball in the house:

Dad: "Hey son, Come here. I'm afraid that dribbling your basketball in the house will hurt the floor, and besides that, it's really annoying."

Son: "It won't hurt the floor."

Dad: Treats the response like annoying behavior and ignores it. "We talked about no dribbling in the house. From now on, if you forget, I will remind you by taking your basketball for as long as I want."

Son: "Seriously?"

Dad: That's all I wanted to tell you.

Son: "What? That's a bunch of crap."

Dad: Says nothing.

Son: "What if I forget and accidentally dribble it?

Dad: "I guess you'll find out."

Son: "Fine!" and stomps away.

If the son continues to argue, the dad can calmly say, "I'm not going to argue about it." If the son still continues to argue, the dad can walk away. Notice that dad ignored anything the boy said that wasn't an effort to clarify the consequence.

After the rule and consequence have been explained, dad will look for good behavior and reward it. "Son, I noticed you didn't dribble your basketball in the house all day. Thank you." The next day however, the son is caught dribbling the basketball in the house.

Dad: "Hey, I see you dribbling you basketball."

Son: "Oh my gosh, really?"

Dad: "I'll take that, thank you."

Son: Throws dad the ball and walks away mad.

Dad: Treats his son's remark as annoying behavior and ignores it. Dad does not say, "Hey, I warned you." or "It was your choice." He keeps the ball for 10 minutes, then finds his son and tosses him the ball. Not a word is said.

Consequences speak so much louder than words. No need to say, "Try to remember from now on," or "Next time it will be longer." If the incident happens again, dad will take the ball for an hour. Then, the next time it happens, maybe all day. It won't be long before the son knows dad is serious when he makes a rule with a consequence. After a couple of days of obeying the rule, dad rewards the good behavior again: "Son, I've notice you haven't dribbled in the house for two days. Thank you." When the son replies with, "Whatever," the dad ignores it as he would any annoying behavior.

Offering Choices with Consequences

Use this technique to make a rule with a consequence in the heat of the moment when there is no time for teaching. For example, you have guests over and your son has been running through the house, back and forth, almost crashing into people and being a nuisance.

In situations like this, I've heard parents say to another adult, "My goodness, he's hyper today." Then the parent will make a half-hearted attempt at changing the behavior: "Brice, stop running, now!" The child ignores the request, and continues to ignore future requests.

Here's the better way: "Brice, stop! Now listen, this is important. No running. Here are your choices. You can walk, or you can spend 10 minutes in your room. You decide." No need to add, "And I mean it."

Now, watch for good behavior and reward it. "Brice. I notice you've been walking." Then give a thumbs-up.

If Brice runs through the house again, mom will calmly say, "Brice, come here. I see you've chosen to go to your room. I will set the timer on the stove for 10 minutes. When it goes off, I will come get you." Mom will treat Brice's whining, begging and pleading the same as she would treat any annoying behavior by completely ignoring it. "But mom, I promise I won't run again. I promise! Please?" to which mom will show neither attention nor emotion. Mom will set the timer, make sure Brice goes to his room, and let the consequence do all the teaching.

When mom goes to release Brice from his room, all she needs to say is, "Your 10 minutes are up."

One caution: do not give in to the pleadings. If you do, you will be teaching your child that pleading equals no consequences, and the next time (and there will be a next time) the pleadings will become louder and longer.

Here is a common situation around the dinner table.

"I want you to eat your vegetables. Here are your choices. You can eat your vegetables, or you can go without dessert. You decide" No need threaten or remind. If the child chooses to ignore the vegetables and they go uneaten, simply do not serve dessert to that child. Let the consequence do all the talking. Do not say anything. You might want to say, "I told you, either eat your vegetables or go without dessert. But you chose not to eat them so enjoy the consequence, pal," but don't!

166

A mom is at the supermarket, shopping. Her child is running all around the store. "Son," she says to him, "No running around in the store. Here are your choices. You can stay by me, or you can sit in the cart. You decide." If the boy continues to run around, she will say, "I see you've decided to sit in the cart."

The purpose of consequences is to allow kids to learn from their mistakes. There is no harm, physically or emotionally like there is in punishment. There is no learning in punishment, other than learning not to get caught next time. Consequences focus on future behavior. Punishment focuses on past behavior. With consequences, there are no surprises.

Your children will not enjoy consequences, but they will think harder before breaking the rule again, and as a result, their behavior will improve much more quickly than with lectures, reminders, threats, and punishment. Kids can blame only themselves when having to endure a consequence and the consequence does all the teaching so mom and dad don't have to.

Chapter 16 – Stop, Redirect, Reward

Sometimes bad behavior becomes more serious than annoying behavior and cannot be ignored, such as a child doing something harmful to another person - whether it be physical or verbal, or a child breaking something or in danger of breaking something. In this example, seven-year-old Brett is angrily screaming at his younger brother David.

First, **STOP** the behavior. Calmly and immediately stop the screaming by taking Brett gently by the arm and moving him a safe distance from his brother David.

Look him squarely in the eye and say calmly but firmly, "You must stop doing that immediately. Screaming is not allowed here."

Then, **REDIRECT** the behavior. Redirect the boy's behavior to something else: "Now sit over here and look at your book," or "Go play with your toys in the other room" or "Go to your room for a few minutes until you feel better. When you are feeling better, come see me". This is where you teach good behavior. Remember, it isn't enough to simply stop the behavior. The behavior must be stopped and then redirected to a better behavior. This is important for two reasons: First, it gets the child doing something other than screaming at his brother. Second, it gets him doing something worthy of a reward.

Then **REWARD** the child for good behavior. After the child has been behaving properly for a few minutes, you have the opportunity to reward good behavior.

When Brett returns, you can say, "Would you like to talk about it?" If he doesn't, then let it go. If he does,

168

use your listening skills you learned in Chapter 7, Acknowledge Negative Feelings. During your conversation, do not get sucked into a conversation about whose fault it was or how unfair it was. Listen, but do not acknowledge anyone's fault. Focus on his feelings. If the little brother wants to talk about it, follow the same procedure with him.

Parents are forever telling their children to "Stop that!", but not providing something else for them to do. When parents tell their children what NOT to do, children focus their attention on the moment, not on what they could do instead.

It is important to direct the child's behavior toward doing something that is good. Then give the child POSITIVE attention (a reward) for the good behavior. "You've been playing with your toys very nicely. Thank you." Then you gently touch his arm.

Now, regarding the younger brother David, who was left crying.

If the child is not hurt, gently touch him, and say, "You will feel better soon." Then very calmly, go on to do something else. Do not show that you are at all upset by the hitting. Treat his crying as annoying behavior and ignore it.

Watch for good behavior from both children and reward it.

After another minute or two, revisit Brett and reward his good behavior by saying, "Thank you, Brett, for being kind to your brother." Then revisit David, and if he has stopped crying, reward him by saying, "You're playing so nicely."

The behavior that receives the most attention is the behavior that will happen the most. Here's another example.

Hitting – Stop, Redirect, Reward

Mom was at home with the children when the four-year-old Jimmy hit the two-year-old Tommy hard enough to require Mom's attention.

She quickly, but calmly, took the four-year-old gently by his arm, led him over to the kitchen table and sat down. She looked him in the eye and said calmly but firmly, "No! You may not do that to your bother. I'm sorry he upset you. Still, no hitting."

"But he started it!" screamed the boy.

Mom ignored his comment. "You may not do that to your bother," She repeated slowly and calmly. "Now you sit up here and color for a while."

The four-year-old sat on the kitchen chair, grabbed a crayon and threw it across the room. "He's always getting me in trouble!" he screamed. Mom completely ignored his annoying behavior. She walked over to the two-year-old who was still crying, and holding his arms out, hoping for a hug. Mom couldn't see any need for first aid. His crying appeared to be for attention only, not because he was hurt. She gave him a pat on the head and said, "You'll feel better soon." and then walked away.

Mom didn't want to reward the crying child with hugs because that would show him that he can get attention by crying. She would rather reward him with a hug for stopping his crying. She'll keep an eye on him and reward him when he stops crying.

170

The two-year-old continued to cry. Mom ignored him.

Mom watched the four-year-old out of the corner of her eye. When he settled down she walked over to him and said, "I like the pictures you color. Will you color one for me?" Then she gave him a hug.

When the two-year-old stopped crying, she walked over to him. He was still lying on the floor. "You've stopped crying. I'm so glad you feel better," then she gave him a hug.

She continued to reward their good behavior. When they started to play nicely together she said to both of them, "You boys are playing nicely together." A few minutes later, she said to the four-year-old, "Thank you for being so kind to your brother."

When the victim of an offense sits crying, holding his arms out to you for comfort, you have to decide, is this just a plea for my attention or is he really hurt? Use your parenting instincts to decide if you should cuddle him or ignore his behavior. How do you know when to ignore and when to pay attention? I can't tell you that. As you experiment with both ways, you should get a feel for which works best in any given situation. Isn't parenting fun?

The Child Ignores Your Request

Dad was fixing a snack for the children. Beth was painting at the table. "Beth, go wash your hands," Dad said. "Just a minute," said Beth. Dad waited a few seconds. Beth kept painting.

Dad calmly walked over to Beth, gently took the paint brush from her hand and pointed to the bathroom.

"Oh man, I'm almost done!" complained Beth.

Dad said nothing. He continued to point to the bathroom. Beth got up and went to wash her hands.

When Beth returned, Dad said, "I know you're really busy, so thank you for doing as I asked." Dad was sure to compliment Beth whenever she did what he asked especially when it was not convenient. He knows that if children expect you to ask more than once, they will always put you off.

Q. You ask Justin to bring his bike in because it looks like rain. He is watching a video and says, "Just a sec." What do you do?

A. After about 10 or 15 seconds, calmly walk over and stand in front of the TV.

Q. Joey is playing his video game. You tell him it's time to get in bed. He says, "In a minute." what do you do?

A. After 10 or 15 seconds, walk over to him and gently take the game away. It might be good to give him a 5 minute warning or say, "It's time to get in bed. Do you want to get in bed now or in 5 minutes?"

Q. Mindy left a mess on the floor. She's about to go next door with her friend. You ask her to clean up before she leaves. She leaves without cleaning. What do you do?

A. Walk next door and get Mindy. Bring her back to clean. If you are watching other small children, take them all with you.

Always reward children for doing what you ask. Whether they do it the first time or the second time you ask, reward them when they finish. They need to know their effort (even if it was given grudgingly) was appreciated.

Chapter 17 – Tantrums

Tantrums are very obnoxious behaviors of young children, but are usually easy to eliminate. When a child has a tantrum, he screams, cries, falls to the floor, kicks, throws his arms around, and is almost impossible to ignore.

What Causes Tantrums?

Tantrums are usually caused by a child not getting what he wants. It works like this: A child wants something: a cookie right before dinner, for instance. His parent tells him "No." So, out of disappointment, the child cries. During one of those times, a parent says, "Ok, stop crying, here's a cookie." What has the child just learned? Crying equals cookie. What a marvelous discovery.

The parent doesn't want the child to get his way every time he cries, so the parent holds out, not giving in when the child asks for a cookie again. The child cries harder. Finally, the parent can't stand the noise any longer and gives the child what he wants.

The parent decides not to give in the next time, but the child doesn't give up. The child has learned that crying long and loud equals cookie.

The longer and louder the tantrum lasts, the more apt the parent is to give into the child's demand. The child learns that he can use the same trick to get candy, toys, even his parent's undivided attention. And it works beautifully at stores, at church, at school, and when visiting friends with mom or dad.

So that's how tantrums get started. If a parent knows what to do, tantrums should never be a problem. Let's look at how you should deal with tantrums. There are three kinds of tantrums:

1. Almost-tantrums

2. Small tantrums

3. Full-blown tantrums

Almost-tantrums

Almost-tantrums are whining, begging and crying. Never give a child what he wants when he is whining, begging or crying for it. When a child whines, begs or cries to get his way, you must absolutely not give in and give the child what he is whining, begging or crying for. Giving in will teach the child that he can get what he wants by whining, begging or crying. You can say, "When you can talk with a sweet voice, then I will talk with you." Then ignore.

Small Tantrums

Small tantrums are just that, small tantrums. The child is not crying or kicking very hard and it looks like it might not last very long. Whatever you do, don't give the child what he wants. Remember, the child is having a tantrum because he was able to get what he wanted in the past by acting this way.

Full-Blown Tantrums

Full-blown tantrums are when the child does not hold back. He throws himself on the floor, kicks hard, screams loudly and seems to be out of control. The child has probably had success using tantrums before and is determined to outlast your resolve to not give in.

What to do

Give an Ignore Warning. While your child is calm, say, "Honey, I want to tell you something. You know how sometimes when you want something and I tell you 'No', and you feel mad and scream and cry and kick your legs? Well, from now on, when you do that, I'm going to ignore you. That means I will pretend that you are not there. It's not that I don't care, I do. And I'll be glad to talk with you after you're feeling better. So, next time you get mad and scream and cry and kick your legs, what am I going to do? That's right. I will ignore you. But I will still love you."

Then, when the child whines, begs, cries or throws a small or a full-blown tantrum because they want something they can't have, stay very calm and give in fantasy what you can't give in reality (See Chapter 11, Enforcing Rules.) Say, "I know, you wish you could have a cupcake, and I wish I could give you all the cupcakes you want, but you're just going to have to wait until after dinner." Then do the following:

Totally ignore the child. Stay calm. Pay no attention to him. Allow the child to kick and scream. Act as if you don't even know he is there. If he grabs your leg, free yourself with as little bother as possible. If the child is in a safe place, leave the room and go where the child can't get to you. Treat this as you would any annoying behavior.

If the child calms down and asks for something in a normal voice, that is, without whining, begging or crying, AND it is okay for him to have it, be sure to compliment him. Say, "You asked me with your very best voice. Good going!" If it is not okay for him to have it, say, "You asked me with your very best voice. Good going. But I'm sorry. You may not have it."

Relocate the child if necessary. If you are at a store, in a restaurant, in church or any other public place, you may feel it necessary to relocate the screaming child. As inconvenient as it may be, remove the child to a safe place. If you are at a restaurant, you might have to sit in the car with your child until everyone else finishes eating. If at a store or church, you may have to go home. The child will come to realize that the tantrum is not going to get him what he wants.

As soon as kids learn that tantrums do not work, the tantrums will stop. Children will do only what works. If tantrums no longer work, there's really no reason to continue using them.

About the Author

When I was a young parent, I had a reoccurring thought about being a parent. It went something like this: "What did I get myself into? This is not what I signed up for. If things don't change, I'm in trouble and so are my kids." You see, I figured that love and common sense and natural instincts were all I needed to raise children. I had observed other parents struggling to "control" their children, and I vowed that would never be me. My kids were going to be cooperative. You can guess what happened. Reality is a hard master. I came to understand and appreciate how those struggling parents felt as I joined their ranks.

I was frustrated by my children's behavior. I thought if I just hung in there and endured, things would change. Then something happened to make me realize that if my kids were going to change, I would have to change first. One evening my wife, my two daughters (ages 3 and 4) and I were sitting down to dinner. We were having the usual drama and chaos that accompanied our meals, but for some reason I wasn't in the mood for it. One of my daughters complained that she didn't get as much mashed potatoes as her sister. Something in me snapped. I put my hand into the bowl of mashed potatoes, scooped out a handful, and threw it down on her plate with a splat. I said, "Happy now?" My daughter cried and I angrily left the table. Up until now I was a nice guy, kind and considerate. My daughters had made me into a monster. I knew something had to change, and soon, before something worse happened.

My wife and I decided to buy a book on parenting. You'd think that would be a pretty simple task, but there were so many books, it was confusing. Did they all teach the same thing or were they all different? If they all taught the same thing, then why so many? If they were all different, then which one was the best? We finally settled on a book called Children the Challenge, by Rudolf Dreikurs. It was green so we called it the "Green Book". My wife and I would constantly ask each other, "What does the Green Book have to say about that?" It was a long book by our standards, and took us a while to read. But over the following months and years it gave us direction, something we had gone without for too long.

Fast forward 25 years. I have six children now, all grown up, some having started families of their own. One day, another life-changing moment occurred. I tell that story in the beginning of Chapter 1. This experience caused me to remember back to the days when I was at the end of my rope as a parent. It made me wonder how many parents were in the same boat that I used to be in – wanting to make a change, but not knowing where to begin.

I thought if I were in their shoes, here is what I would want. I would want a book that promises to bring out the best in me and my children. I would want that book to be short and to the point, easy to understand and easy to do. I would want that book to contain the best parts out of the best books. So I set out to create such a book.

It took me about three years. During that time I read a lot about child behavior. Often, my book would be the last thing I would think about before falling to sleep at night, and the first thing on my mind when I woke up in the morning. Many times I'd wake up in the middle of the night with a thought that I had to write down or I could not go back to sleep. I carried a pen and paper with me everywhere to capture the fleeting moments of inspiration.

I was constantly deciding what information to include in my book and what information to leave out. I struggled at putting into words exactly what I wanted to say. Even though I've written, I don't consider myself a writer; more of an information giver.

While I was at the keyboard I had what I like to think of as metaphysical or "spiritual" experiences. I always prayed before I sat down to write. I guess I felt like I could use all the help I could get. I felt like there were people who were close by that I couldn't see, perhaps ancestors of mine who had died, whose spirits were around me, wanting to help. So I talked to them. I'd say out loud, "Okay you guys, I'm having some trouble here. I could use some help." Then I would stop trying to think, and wait. After a moment, three or four words would come to my mind. I'd say, "Go on," and the thought would come, "Just start typing!" So I would, and after I had typed those three or four words, another few words would come to mind, and this would continue until I had completed a whole paragraph.

I'm telling you this because I want to share with you what compelled me to finish this book during discouraging times. (And, if something doesn't look right, it's not all my fault.)

This book is short compared to other books on the subject. It's meant to be that way. So, I'd be very interested in your feedback:

- Is there something *you* do to improve your children's behavior that this book does not address?

- Do you have a question or concern this book did not cover?

- Is there something in this book you don't agree with?

- Can you share an experience where this book has helped you?

As I look at it, we're all in this raising-kids-thing together. We are the "village" helping each other to raise children. I can make a collection of your comments and publish them. So please, email them to me.

It is my sincere hope that this book will give you the help that you've been looking for. It has truly been a labor of love for me.

Richard O'Keef
howtogetkidstobehave@gmail.com

Notes

Chapter 3

1 Jane Nelsen, Ed.D., *Positive Discipline*, 3rd ed. (New York: Ballantine Books, 2006), p. 14.

Chapter 4

1 Dr. Glenn I. Latham, *The Power of Positive Parenting* (P & T ink, 1990), p. 9.

2 Paul Axtell, *Ten Powerful Things to Say to Your Kids: Creating the relationship you want with the most important people in your life* (Jackson Creek Press, 2011), p. 33-34.

3 Dale Carnegie, How to Win Friends & Influence People (New York: Pocket Books, 1936), p.5

Chapter 6

1 Stephen R. Covey, *The 7 Habits of Highly Effective Families* (New York: Golden Books, 1997), p. 45.

Chapter 7

1 Adele Faber & Elaine Mazlish, *How To Talk So Kids Will Listen & How To Listen So Kids Will Talk* (New York: Scribner, 2012), p.42

Chapter 8

1 Merrilee Brown Boyack, *The Parenting Breakthrough* (Deseret Book Company, 2005), p. 12.

Chapter 11

1 Dr. Haim G. Ginott, *Between Parent and Child* (New York: Three Rivers Press, 1965, Revised and

updated by Dr. Alice Giinott and Dr. H. Wallace Goddard, 2003), p. 87.

2 Jane Nelsen, Lynn Lott, and H. Stephen Glenn, *Positive Discipline A-Z: 1001 Solutions to Everyday Parenting Problems*, 3rd ed. (New York: Three Rivers Press, 2007), p. 4.

Chapter 12
1 Amy McCready, *If I Have to Tell You One More Time* (New York: Penguin Group, 2012), p. 138.

Chapter 14
1 Adele Faber & Elaine Mazlish, *Siblings Without Rivalry* (New York: W. W. Norton& Company, Inc, 2012), p.157

33066111R00109

Made in the USA
San Bernardino, CA
23 April 2016